Edward III & his Wars, 1327-1360

ENGLISH HISTORY BY CONTEMPORARY WRITERS.

THE series, of which the present volume is one, aims at setting forth the facts of our National History, political and social, in a way not yet systematically tried in this country, but somewhat like that which Messrs. Hachette have successfully wrought out in France under the editorship of MM. Zeller, Darsy, Luchaire, etc. It is planned not only for educational use but for the general reader, and especially for all those to whom the original contemporary authorities are for various reasons difficult of access.

To each well-defined period of our history is given a little volume made up of extracts from the chronicles, state papers, memoirs, and letters of the time, as also from other contemporary literature, the whole chronologically arranged and chosen so as to give a living picture of the effect produced upon each generation by the political, religious, social, and intellectual movements in which it took part.

Extracts from foreign tongues are Englished, and passages from old English authors put into modern spelling, but otherwise as far as may be kept in original form. When needed a glossary is added and brief explanatory notes. To each volume is also appended a short account of the writers quoted and of their relations to the events they describe, as well as such tables and summaries as may facilitate reference. Such illustrations as are given are chosen in the same spirit as the text, and represent monuments, documents, sites, portraits, coins, etc.

The chief aim of the series is to send the reader to the best original authorities, and so to bring him as close as may be to the mind and feelings of the times he is reading about.

No definite chronological system of issue is adopted, but it is hoped that the entire period of Mediæval and Renaissance history may be covered in the space of two or three years.

F. YORK POWELL,

Editor of the Series.

Ch. Ch., Oxford, 1887.

ENGLISH HISTORY BY CONTEMPORARY
WRITERS

Edward iij & his Wars

1327—1360

Extracts from the Chronicles of Froissart, Jehan le
Bel, Knighton, Adam of Murimuth, Robert
of Avesbury, the Chronicle of Lanercost,
the State Papers, & other contemporary
records

ARRANGED AND EDITED BY

W. J. ASHLEY, M.A.

Fellow of Lincoln College, Oxford

LONDON

DAVID NUTT

1887

BEDFORD:

ARTHUR RANSOM, PRINTER, HIGH STREET.

PREFACE.

THE age of Edward III. is the age of chivalry.
This is alike its praise and its condemnation.
Those who care for history because of the bright
pictures it brings before them, the moving
incident, the gallant feat, will delight in the
pages of Froissart and ask no more: while to
others the warriors of the 14th century will
seem too often mean or selfish; they will ask
rather what was the life of the people or the
development of the constitution. The extracts
here collected will, it is hoped, be interesting
to both classes. Battles and campaigns take
up, it is true, the larger part of the book, but
this is fitting; for it tells the story of the great
struggle with the kings of France which had
such far-reaching consequences to the two
countries. But the constitutional and social
results of the period have also been as far as

possible illustrated. Narratives of Crecy and Poitiers, of Halidon Hill and Neville's Cross will be found here; but so will also the statutes for the protection of the English church and concerning taxation and treason, some account of the Black Death and its consequences, some glimpses into the history of industry and the life of the universities.

In the appendix are given a description of the authors herein used and various genealogical tables; it may be well to mention also that the headings to the extracts are in almost every case taken from the original authorities. It remains only for the editor to express his gratitude to Miss Lucy Hill for much careful assistance and many a happy suggestion.

Lincoln College, February, 1887.

EDWARD III & HIS WARS

1327.—The accession of Edward III.

Murimuth, 51-53.

(Queen Isabella and the young prince Edward, who had been in France negotiating about Guienne, returned to England in September, 1326, accompanied by Mortimer and a force of Hainaulters, their declared purpose being to put an end to the misrule of the Despensers. They met with no opposition; the Despensers were hanged; and Edward II. was imprisoned at Kenilworth.)

The queen (Isabella) . . . immediately after Epiphany, caused a parliament to be held, in which it was ordained, on behalf of the whole realm, that three bishops, two earls, two abbots, and four barons, from each county of England two knights, also from London and the other cities and great towns, and especially from the Cinque Ports, a certain number of persons, should be sent to the king (Edward II.) at Kenilworth, and should tell him and diligently require him to resign the royal dignity and crown, and permit his eldest son to reign in his stead; otherwise they would return him their homages and elect another as their king. When he heard this, the king replied, with weeping and lamentation, that it grieved him much that he had deserved so ill of his people; but, since it could not be otherwise, said he, he was glad that his son had been thus received by the whole people, and that he should succeed him and reign in his stead. Then the delegates, returning to the parliament at London, reported the king's answers fully, more fully indeed than they had been given; and when they had heard them the whole community of the realm at once admitted the young Edward as king, and on the first day of February caused him to be crowned at Westminster by archbishop Walter. . . Moreover, such and so great a dowry was assigned to the queen that scarcely a third part of the realm remained to the king, her son.

SEAL OF EDWARD III.

1327.—Charter granting the township of Southwark to the citizens of London.

Inserted in the London *Liber Custumarum* (in *Munimenta Gildhallæ Londoniensis*, ii. 435. Rolls Series).

(This important grant to the citizens of London was probably given as a reward for their support in the recent revolution.)

Edward, by the grace of God, king of England, lord of Ireland, and duke of Aquitaine, to all to whom the present letters may come, greeting.

Know that whereas our beloved citizens of our city of London, by their petition shewn to us and our council in our present parliament at Westminster assembled, have given us to understand that felons, robbers, and divers other malefactors and disturbers of the peace, who have committed in that city and elsewhere murders, robberies, and divers other felonies, secretly leave that city after committing such felonies and take refuge in the township of Southwark, where they cannot be arrested by the officers of the said city, and are there publicly received; and so, from want of due punishment, they are made the more bold in committing like felonies; and have besought us, for the preservation of our peace in the said city, and bridling the malice of these criminals, to grant them the said township, to have to themselves, their heirs and successors for ever, in return for a ferm (annual payment) due therefor to be annually paid to us at our Exchequer —We, having consideration to the foregoing, by the consent of the prelates, earls, barons, and commons of our realm in the present parliament, grant for us and our heirs, to the same citizens, the said township of Southwark, with what thereto pertains, to have and to hold to them, their heirs and successors, the citizens of the said city, of us and our heirs for ever, paying to us annually at the Exchequer of us and our heirs, at the accustomed terms, the ferm thereof due and accustomed. In witness of which we have caused these, our Letters Patent, to be drawn up. Witness myself at Westminster, the sixth day of March, the first year of our reign.

1327.—Here the history speaketh of the manner of the Scots and how they can war.

Froissart, ch. 17 (I. § 28). *Jehan le Bel*, ch. 10.

(Robert Bruce took advantage of the troubles in England upon the deposition of Edward II. to break the truce and send an army to ravage the northern counties. Jehan le Bel accompanied the English force against them, and thus describes the Scotch troops.)

These Scottish men are right hardy and sore travailing in harness and in wars. For when they will enter into England, within a day and a night they will drive their whole host twenty-four miles. For they are all a-horse-back, without it be the camp-followers who come on foot. The knights and squires are well horsed, and the common people and others on little hackneys and geldings ; and they carry with them no carts nor chariots, for the diversities of the mountains that they must pass through in the county of Northumberland. They take with them no purveyance of bread or wine ; for their usage and soberness is such, in the time of war, that they will pass in the journey a great long time with flesh half sodden, without bread, and drink of the river water without wine ; and they neither care for pots nor pans, for they seethe beasts in their own skins. They are ever sure to find plenty of beasts in the country that they will pass through. Therefore they carry with them none other purveyance, but on their horse between the saddle and the panel they truss a broad plate of metal, and behind the saddle they will have a little sack full of oatmeal to the intent that, when they have

eaten of the sodden flesh, then they lay this plate
on the fire and mix a little oatmeal, and when the
plate is hot they cast of the thin paste thereon,
and so make a little cake in manner of a cracknel
or biscuit, and that they eat to comfort withal their
stomachs. Wherefore it is no great marvel though
they make greater journeys than other people do.
And in this manner were the Scots entered into the
said country, and wasted and burnt all about as they
went, and took a great number of the beasts. They
were to the number of four thousand men of arms,
knights and squires, mounted on good horses, and
other ten thousand men of war were armed after
their manner, right hardy and fierce, mounted on
little hackneys, the which were never tied nor kept
at hard meat, but let go to pasture in the fields
and bushes.

1327.—How the English sought the Scots and knew not where they were.

Froissart, ch. 18 (I. §§ 30, 31, 32). *Jehan le Bel*, ch. 11, 12.

(The English, being unable to find the Scots, tried to cut
off their retreat.)

. . . It was determined by great advice and
counsel that all the host should remove at midnight,
and make haste in the morning, to the intent to stop
the passage of the river of Tyne from the Scots,
whereby they should be advised by force, either to
fight with them, or else to abide still in England
to their great danger and loss. And to this con-
clusion all the host was accorded, and so supped

and lodged as well as they might that night, and every man was warned to be ready at the first sounding of the trumpet, and at the second blast every man to arm himself without delay, and at the third every man quickly to mount on his horse and to draw under his own standard and banner, and every man to take with him but one loaf of bread, and to truss it behind him on his horse. It was also determined that they should leave behind them all their loose harness and all manner of carriages and provisions; for they thought surely to fight with the Scots the next day, whatsoever danger they were in, thinking to jeopard either to win or to lose all. And thus it was ordained and so it was accomplished, for about midnight every man was ready apparelled. Few had slept but little, and yet they had sore travailed the day before. Great haste as they made, ere they were arranged in battle-array the day began to appear. Then they advanced forward in all haste, through mountains, valleys, and rocks, and through many evil passages without any plain country. And on the highest of these hills and on the plain of these valleys there were marvellous great marshes and dangerous passages, that it was great marvel that much people had not been lost; for they rode ever still forward and never tarried one for another; for whosoever fell in any of these marshes with much pain could they get any aid to help them out again. So that in diverse places there were many lost and especially horses and carriages. And often times in the day there was cried alarm, for it

was said ever that the foremost company of their
host were fighting with their enemies; so that the
hindermost thought it had been true, wherefore they
hasted them over rocks and stones and mountains
with helm and shield ready apparelled to fight, with
spear and sword ready in hand without tarrying for
father, brother, or companion. And when they had
thus run forth often times in the day the space of
half-a-mile together toward the crying, thinking it
had been their enemies, they were deceived, for the
cry ever arose by the raising of harts, hinds, and
other savage beasts that were seen by them in the
forward; after the which beasts they made such
shouting and crying, that they that came after
thought they had been fighting with their enemies.
Thus rode forth all that day the young king of
England by mountains and deserts without finding
any highway, town, or village. And when it was
again night they came to the river Tyne. . . .

(They crossed the river, and waited in the rain and with little
food till the middle of next day; but the Scots did not appear.)
About noon some poor folks of the country were
found, and they said how they were then fourteen
miles from Newcastle-upon-Tyne and eleven miles
from Carlisle. . . . . And when this was shewn
to the king and to the lords of his council,
immediately were sent thither horses and sumpters
to fetch thence some purveyance; and there was
a cry in the king's name made in the town of
Newcastle that whosoever would bring bread or
wine or any other victual, should be paid therefor

immediately at a good price, and they should be
conducted to the host in safeguard; for it was
published openly that the king and his host would
not depart from the place they were in till they
had some tidings where their enemies were. And
the next day by noon such as had been sent for
victual returned again to the host, with such purveyance as they could get, and that was not over
much; and with them came other folks of the
country with little nags charged with bread, evil
baked in panniers, and small pear wine in barrels,
and other victual, to sell in the host, whereby great
part of the host were well refreshed and eased. And
thus they continued, day by day, the space of eight
days, awaiting every day the returning again of the
Scots, who knew no more where the English host
lay than they knew where the Scots were; so each
of them were ignorant of the other. . . . . .
Thus three days and three nights they were in
manner without bread, wine, candle, or light, fodder
or forage, or any manner of provision either for horse
or man. And after the space of four days a loaf
of bread was sold for six pennies the which was
worth but one penny, and a gallon of wine for six
groats that was worth but six pennies. And yet for
all that, there was such rage of famine that each took
victuals out of others' hands, whereby there arose
divers battles and strifes between sundry companions;
and yet beside all these mischiefs it never ceased to
rain all the whole week, whereby their saddles,
panels, and saddlestraps were all rotten and broken

and most part of their horses hurt on their backs; nor they had not wherewith to shoe them that were unshod; nor they had nothing to cover themselves withal from the rain and cold, but green bushes and their armour. Nor they had nothing to make fire withal but green boughs, the which would not burn because of the rain. . . . .

(The Scots not appearing, the English recrossed the river and tried to find them.)

. . . Again, the fourth day they rode forth in like manner till it was about the hour of three, and there came a squire fast riding toward the king and said, "An it like your grace, I have brought you perfect tidings of the Scots, your enemies; surely they be within three miles of you, lodged on a great mountain, abiding there for you. . . . Sir, this that I show you is of truth, for I approached so near to them that I was taken prisoner, and brought before the lords of their host, and there I shewed them tidings of you, and how that ye seek for them, to the intent to have battle, and the lords did quit me my ransom and prison, when I had shewed them how our grace had promised a hundred pounds sterling of rent to him that brought first tiding of them to you; and they made me to promise that I should not rest until I had shewed you these tidings, for they said they had as great desire to fight with you as you had with them." . . . .

(The English followed this squire and found the Scots strongly posted on a hill with a river running in front, and refusing to leave their strong position.)

. . . And there were heralds of arms sent to
the Scots, giving them knowledge that if they would
come and pass the river to fight with them in the
plain field, they would draw back from the river
and give them sufficient place to arrange their lines
of battle, either the same day or else the next, as
they should choose themselves, or else to let them
do likewise and they would come over to them.
And when the Scots heard this they took counsel
among themselves; and anon they answered the
heralds how they would do neither the one nor the
other, and said, "Sirs, your king and his lords
see well how we be here in this realm, and have
burnt and wasted the country as we have passed
through; and if they be displeased therewith, let
them amend it when they will, for here we will
abide so long as it shall please us." . . . .
And between the day and the night, they made a
marvellous great noise with blowing of horns all at
once, that it seemed properly that all the devils
of hell had been there. Thus these two hosts
were lodged there that night, the which was St.
Peter's night, in the beginning of August, the
year of our Lord, 1327. . . . .

(After facing one another for five days, the Scots departed
in the night; the English again found them, and the same
comedy was played.)

The first night that the English host was thus
lodged on the second mountain, the lord James
Douglas took with him about two hundred men
of arms, and passed the river far off from the

host so that he was not perceived; and suddenly he brake into the English host about midnight, crying, "Douglas! Douglas! Ye shall all die, thieves of England"; and he slew or seized 300 men, some in their beds and some scant ready; and he strake his horse with the spurs, and came to the king's own tent, always crying "Douglas!" and strake asunder two or three cords of the king's tent, and so departed, and in the retreat he lost some of his men. . . . .

(Again the Scots eluded them.)

Then the English lords said it were but a folly to follow the Scots, for they saw well they could not overtake them. . . . . And divers of the English host mounted on their horses, and passed over the river and came to the mountain where the Scots had been, and there they found more than 500 great beasts ready slain, because the Scots could not drive them before their host, and because that the Englishmen should have but small profit of them; also there they found 300 cauldrons made of beast's skins with the hair still on them, strained on stakes over the fire, full of water and full of flesh to be sodden; and more than a thousand spits full of flesh to be roasted; and more than ten thousand old shoes made of new leather with the hair still on them, the which the Scots had left behind them; also there they found five poor Englishmen, bound fast to certain trees and some of their legs broken; these they loosed and let go and then they returned again.

2

By that time all the host was dislodged; and it was ordained by the king, and by the advice of his council, that the whole host should follow the marshal's banners and draw homeward into England.

1327.—The murder of Edward II.

Murimuth, 53-55.

Because it seemed to some that lord Edward, father of the king, was too delicately treated at Kenilworth, it was ordered that lord Thomas of Berkeley and lord John of Mautravers should have the custody of him; wherefore, about Palm Sunday, he was secretly taken to Berkeley. And, because they feared that some would come to free him, he was taken from that place by night to divers places, viz., to Corf and to some other secret places, but finally they brought him back to Berkeley, so that he could scarce know where he was; and the lord of Berkeley, who behaved humanely towards him, had always charge of him for one month, and the next month lord John Mautravers, who behaved towards him differently. The queen, indeed, sent him delicate raiment and courteous letters, but would not see him, pretending that the community of the realm would not permit her. He had an allowance, viz., a hundred marks a month; and so at Berkeley and elsewhere, not where he pleased but where this John Mautravers pleased, he lived as best he could until the time to be mentioned below. . . . Afterwards, on the 21st of September, in the

year of Our Lord, 1327, Edward, king of England, died
in the castle of Berkeley, wherein, as I have before
said, he was imprisoned or unwillingly detained.
And, although many abbots, priors, knights, burgesses of Bristol and Gloucester, had been summoned
to see that his body was unhurt, and had superficially
seen it, yet it was commonly said that he had been
killed as a precaution by the order of the lords
John Mautravers and Thomas of Gorneye, because
these two and some others fled; but Thomas of
Gorneye was three years afterwards recognised and
captured at Marseilles by the procurement of a
certain lady of England, and was sent to England
to suffer the penalty of his misdeeds, but he was
beheaded upon the sea upon some pretext; lest
perchance he should accuse magnates and great
prelates in England of consent and connivance at
the King's death; but lord John Mautravers betook
himself to Germany, and there he abode and abides
still up to the present date.

1328.—How king Edward was married to my lady Philippa of Hainault.

Froissart, ch. 19 (I. §§ 38-9). *Jehan le Bel*, ch. 14.

It was not long after that the king and the queen
his mother, the earl of Kent his uncle, the earl of
Lancaster, sir Roger Mortimer, and all the barons
of England who were of the king's council, sent a
bishop and two knights bannerets with two notable
clerks to sir John of Hainault, praying him to be a
mean that their lord, the young king of England,

might have in marriage one of the daughters of the
earl of Hainault his brother, named Philippa ; for
the king and all the nobles of the realm had rather
have her than any other lady for the love of him.
Sir John of Hainault, lord Beaumont, feasted and
honoured greatly these ambassadors, and brought
them to Valenciennes to the earl his brother, who
honourably received them and made them such cheer
that it were over long here to rehearse. And when
they had shown the contents of their message, the
earl said, " Sirs, I thank greatly the king, your
prince, and the queen his mother, and all other
lords of England, since they have sent such sufficient
personages as ye be to do me such honour as to treat
for the marriage, to the which request I am well
agreed, if our holy father, the pope, will consent
thereto " ; with the which answer these ambassadors
were right well content. Then they sent two
knights and two clerks immediately to the pope
to Avignon, to obtain a dispensation for this
marriage ; for without the pope's license they
might not marry, for in the lineage of France they
were so near of kin as at the third degree, for
the two mothers were cousins german, issued of
two brethren.   And when these ambassadors were
come to the pope, and their requests and considera-
tions well heard, our holy father the pope, with all the
whole college, consented to this marriage, and
so feasted them.   And then they departed and
came again to Valenciennes with their bulls.
Then this marriage was concluded and affirmed

on both parties ; . . . . there this princess was
married, by a sufficient procuration brought from
the king of England; and after all feasts and
triumphs done, then this young queen entered into
the sea at Wysant, and arrived with all her company
at Dover. And sir John of Hainault, lord Beaumont,
her uncle, did conduct her to the city of London
where there was made great feast. . . . . The
English chronicle saith the marriage and coronation
of the queen was done at York, with much honour,
the Sunday in the even of the conversion of S. Paul,
in the year of our Lord 1327. (N.S. 1328.).

1328, March.—Peace with Scotland.

Chronicle of Lanercost, p. 261.

Then the king of England (hearing of the death
of his uncle without heir, and deeming himself of
right the next heir to reign in France, yet fearing
that those of France would not suffer him, but would
choose another of the royal blood to be their king,
as indeed they immediately did, the son, to wit, of
Charles, the uncle of the late king), by the most evil
advice of his mother and lord Roger of Mortimer,
who were the chief leaders of the king who was
scarce fifteen years old, was compelled to give up to
the Scots, by his public charter, every exaction,
right, and claim lately made of chief lordship over
the realm of Scotland, for himself and his heirs for
ever, without their doing homage to the kings of
England. He gave up also to them the piece of the
Cross of Christ, which the Scots call the Blackrood,

and likewise an instrument or charter of subjection
or doing of homage to the kings of England, with
the seals of all the magnates of Scotland hanging
to it, which they had given to the king's grandfather, and which the Scots on account of its many
seals called Ragman.   But the stone of Scone,
whereon the kings of Scotland were wont to be
placed at their coronation, the Londoners would by
no means send away.   All these the famous king
Edward, son of Henry, had caused to be brought
from Scotland when he brought the Scots beneath
his sway.   Moreover the young king gave his
younger sister, lady Joan of the Tower, in marriage
to David, son of Robert Bruce, king of Scotland,
who was then a boy of five years old, as his mother
the queen of England had advised, who at that
time ruled the whole kingdom.   And the marriage
was solemnly celebrated at Berwick, on the Sunday
next before the feast of S. Mary Magdalen.

1328.—How king Robert Bruce of Scotland died.

Froissart, ch. 20 (I. §§ 40-41).   *Jehan le Bel*, ch. 15-16·

In the meantime it fortuned that king Robert of
Scotland was right sore aged and feeble ; for he was
greatly charged with the great sickness (leprosy), so
that there was no way with him but death.   And
when he felt that his end drew near, he sent for
such barons and lords of his realm as he trusted
best, and shewed them how there was no remedy
with him, but he must needs leave this transitory
life; commanding them on the faith and truth that

they owed him, truly to keep the realm and aid
the young prince David his son ; and that when
he was of age they should obey him and crown
him king, and marry him in such a manner as
was convenient for his estate. Then he called to
him the gentle knight, sir James Douglas, and
said before all the lords : " Sir James, my dear
friend, ye know well that I have had much ado
in my days to uphold and sustain the right of this
realm ; and when I had most ado I made a solemn
vow, the which as yet I have not accomplished,
whereof I am right sorry ; the which was, if I might
achieve and make an end of all my wars, so that
I might once have brought this realm in rest and
peace, then I promised in my mind to have gone
and warred on Christ's enemies, the adversaries of
our holy Christian faith. To this purpose mine
heart has ever intended, but our Lord would not
consent thereto ; for I have had so much ado in
my days, and now in my last enterprise I have
taken such a malady that I cannot escape. And
since it is that my body cannot go nor achieve
that my heart desireth, I will send the heart instead
of the body to accomplish my vow. And because
I know in all my realm no knight more valiant
than ye be nor of body so well furnished to
accomplish my vow instead of myself, therefore
I require you, my own dear especial friend, that
ye will take on you this voyage for the love of
me, and to acquit my soul against my Lord God.
For I trust so much in your nobleness and **truth**

that, an ye will take it on you, I doubt not but
that ye shall achieve it, and I declare then shall
I die in more ease and quiet so that it be done
in such manner as I shall declare unto you. I
will that, as soon as I shall be passed out of this
world, ye take my heart out of my body and
embalm it; and take of my treasure as ye shall
think sufficient for that enterprise, both for yourself
and such company as ye will take with you; and
present my heart to the Holy Sepulchre where our
Lord lay, seeing that my body cannot come there.
And take with you such company and purveyance as
shall be appertaining to your estate. And wheresoever ye come, let it be known how ye carry with
you the heart of king Robert of Scotland at his
request and desire, to be presented to the Holy
Sepulchre." Then all the lords that heard these
words wept for pity. And when this knight sir
James Douglas might speak for weeping, he said
"Ah! gentle and noble king, a hundred times I
thank your grace for the great honour that ye do to
me, since of so noble and great treasure ye give me
in charge; and, sir, I shall do with a glad heart all
that ye have commanded me to the best of my true
power; howbeit I am not worthy nor sufficient to
achieve such a noble enterprise." Then the king
said "Ah! gentle knight I thank you, so that ye
will promise to do it." "Sir," said the knight,
"I shall do it undoubtedly, by the faith that I
owe to God and to the order of knighthood."
"Then I thank you," said the king, "for now shall

I die in more ease of my mind, since that I know
that the most worthy and sufficient knight of my
realm shall achieve for me that which I could
never attain unto." And thus, soon after this,
noble Robert de Bruce, king of Scotland, passed
away out of this uncertain world. And his heart
was taken out of his body and embalmed, and
honourably he was interred in the Abbey of Dun-
fermline in the year of our Lord God, 1328, the
7th day of the month of November.

And when the spring-time began, then sir James
Douglas purveyed him with that which appertained
for his enterprise and took his ship at the port of
Montrose in Scotland, and sailed into Flanders to
Sluys, to hear tidings and to know if there were any
noble men in that country that would go to Jerusalem,
to the intent to have more company. And he lay
still at Sluys the space of 12 days ere he departed;
but he would never come a-land, but kept still his
ship and always kept his state and behaviour with
great triumph, with trumpets and clarions as though
he had been king of Scots himself. And in his
company there was a knight banneret, and eight
other knights of the realm of Scotland and twenty-
four young squires and gentlemen to serve him.
And all his vessels were of gold and silver, pots,
basins, ewers, dishes, flagons, barrels, cups, and all
other things. And all such as would come and see
him, they were well served with two manner of wines
and divers manner of spices, all manner of people
according to their degrees. And when he had thus

tarried there the space of twelve days, he heard
reported that Alfonso, king of Spain, made war
against a Saracen king of Granada. Then he
thought to join himself to the Spanish king, thinking
surely he could not bestow his time more nobly than
to war against God's enemies. And that enterprise
done, then he thought to go forth to Jerusalem and
to achieve that he was charged with. And so he
departed and took the sea towards Spain, and arrived
at the port of Valencia the great. Then he went
straight to the king of Spain who held his host
against the Saracen king of Granada, and they were
near together on the frontiers of his land. And
within a while after that this knight, sir James
Douglas, was come to the king of Spain, on a day
the king issued out into the field to approach nearer
to his enemies. And the king of Granada issued
out in like wise on his part, so that each king might
see the other with all their banners displayed. Then
they arranged their battles each against the other.
Then sir James Douglas drew out on the one side
with all his company to the intent to show his
prowess the better. And when he saw these battles
thus ranged on both parties, and saw that the battle
of the king of Spain began somewhat to advance
toward their enemies he thought then verily that
they should soon assemble together to fight at hand
strokes ; and then he thought rather to be with the
foremost than with the hindermost, and struck his
horse with his spurs, and all his company also, and
dashed into the battle of the king of Granada,

crying, "Douglas, Douglas!" weening that the king
of Spain and his host had followed, but they did
not; wherefore he was dismayed, for the Spanish
host stood still.   And so this gentle knight was
enclosed and all his company with the Saracens,
where he did marvels in arms, but finally he could
not endure, so that he and all his company were
slain.

1328-9. — Of the struggle between Mortimer and Lancaster.

Knighton, 2554.

At Salisbury, queen Isabella and Roger of Mortimer
made new earls, namely, John of Eltham, earl of
Cornwall; Roger of Mortimer, earl of March;
Edmund Butler, earl of Ormond.   All these, with
their adherents, brought together a great army to
Isabella the queen against Henry earl of Lancaster
and the other magnates of the realm who had not
been consenting to their nefarious deeds.   And they
rode with force and arms upon the lands of the
said earl, and came to Leicester with a great army
of English and Welsh on the fourth of January, and
they remained in Leicester and in the country around
eight days, and spoiled the country everywhere,
woods, parks, vineyards, pools, and fishponds, and
took away with them everything, whether precious
or not, that their hands could find, gold, silver, corn,
tools, beds, tables, arms, clothes, game and cattle,
sheep and oxen, geese and hens, and church
ornaments, leaving nothing that they could find in

churches or elsewhere, as if it had been in time of war between kingdoms.   And all this as an insult to the earl of Lancaster, who was then coming from the eastern counties with a large force, wishing to meet them, having in his following the magnates who had been with Thomas earl of Lancaster, to wit the earl of Norfolk, Edmund earl of Kent, his brother and uncle of the king, the bishops of London and Winchester, the lord Wake, the lord Beaumont, Hugh of Audley, the lord Thomas Rosselyne, and many others.   And when these magnates had made themselves ready for the attack, since they distrusted Roger Mortimer, by whose counsel and prompting the king had taken offence against certain of his faithful lieges, the two uncles of the king, Thomas and Edmund, left the earl and joined the king's mother and Roger Mortimer. . . . . . Earl Henry, trusting in their fidelity, had taken his stand in a field near Bedford, and fixed his tents, purposing to join battle with Roger of Mortimer and his adherents; but, owing to this betrayal, he humbly submitted himself to the king in the field in the presence of the whole army.   And there it was agreed, in the presence of Simon archbishop of Canterbury and other bishops and many of the magnates of the realm, that all evils should be remedied in the next parliament, and this lest, perchance, all the commons should rise and make common cause with the earl.

1330.—Of the death of Edmund of Kent.

Knighton, 2555.

In the year of grace, 1330, and in the 4th year of the reign of king Edward, the king held a parliament at Winchester. In which it was laid to the charge of Edmund earl of Kent by Isabella the mother, and Roger Mortimer and others of their party, that he had endeavoured and taken great pains, contrary to his duty to the king, to free Edward, his brother, formerly king of England, from the castle of Berkeley, to the prejudice and hurt of the crown. Wherefore the said Edmund was taken and imprisoned and condemned to the penalty of beheading; and so stood outside the gate of the castle, awaiting death until the hour of vespers, because no one was willing to behead him, for the pity they had for him, for he had been condemned without common consent. At last came a ribald scoundrel from the Marshalsey, and, to gain his own life, beheaded him on Monday in the vigil of S. Cuthbert.

1330.—Of the fall of Roger Mortimer.

Knighton, 2555-7.

. . . Then a rumour began to spread through the whole of England of the malignity and cruelty of Isabella, the king's mother, and of the many seditions of Roger Mortimer. In the first place that they encouraged the Scots to the great hurt and disgrace of the king and kingdom of England, and how that she had put to death king Edward, once her husband, and how many evils were done in the realm by their counsel and aid, and how many evil works were concealed by their help. Wherefore the king, by the secret advice of his friends, determined to break up their fellowship, lest worse or like should at any time arise by their act or counsel. For they were becoming so strong in the land that the whole kingdom seemed in peril of falling. Then the king held his council at Nottingham in the season of Michaelmas, with almost all the magnates of the realm. Wherein the king, being more wholesomely taught by wiser counsel of their fraud and malice, and seeing the danger as well past as future and present from the said Isabella and Mortimer, was much moved at heart ; and so on the Wednesday on the morrow of S. Luke, the king with a picked following on a dark night made his way by a certain subterranean passage from the town of Nottingham into the castle, and came into the chamber of his mother, Isabella, and found there near her in another chamber Roger Mortimer and Henry, bishop of Lincoln. And immediately the king ordered Roger to be apprehended and put in safe custody until the morrow. On the morrow he caused all his adherents scattered through the whole town to be apprehended. . . . . . And in the capture of Roger Mortimer, Hugh of Tryplington, a knight and seneschal of the king's household, was killed by Roger Mortimer in the entry of the king into their chamber. Isabella, the king's mother, was adjudged to lose all her lands, and with difficulty escaped the sentence of death, this being refrained from because she was the king's mother and on account of the king's reverence. And it was ordained that each year 3,000 marks should be taken from the chest of the king for her sustenance, and that she should dwell where the king should appoint. . . . . Then the king ordered the earls, barons, and other magnates of the realm, to pass just sentence on Roger Mortimer. These all consulting together came and said that all the above articles witnessed against Roger were true and notorious, and known to all the people of the land, especially the article touching the death of the king at Berkeley ; wherefore it was determined and adjudged that the said Roger should be drawn and hanged at London. His body hung bare on the gallows two days and two nights, and was then buried at the convent of the Franciscans at London.

1331.—Protection to a Flemish weaver.

Rymer, *Fœdera*, ii. 823.

(This illustrates the policy of Edward III. to encourage the settlement of foreign weavers in England, to which was chiefly due the rapid growth of the cloth manufacture in England from this time.)

The king to all bailiffs, etc., to whom these letters may come, greeting. Know that, whereas John Kempe, of Flanders, weaver of woollen cloths, has come to dwell within our realm of England for the sake of exercising his craft therein and of instructing and informing those who wish to learn

the same, and has brought with him certain men
and servants and apprentices of that craft:

We take this John, his men, servants, and
apprentices aforesaid, together with all their goods
and chattels, into our protection, and we promise
to other men of that craft, as well as to dyers and
fullers, wishing to come from across the sea to
dwell within our kingdom for the same cause, that
similar letters shall be granted. . . . .

Witness the king, at Lincoln, the 28th day of July.

(Similar letters of protection were afterwards frequently issued,
e.g. to two Brabant weavers who had settled at York in 1336, to
weavers from Zealand in 1337.)

1333.—Of the battle of Halidon Hill.

Chronicle of Lanercost, p. 273.

(The Scotch government having refused to reinstate those
English lords who had lands in Scotland, they induced Edward
Balliol, son of king John Balliol, to make an attempt to gain the
crown in the summer of 1332. At first he was entirely successful; the regent was defeated at Duplin Moor, and Balliol was
crowned at Scone. But in a few months he had to take refuge
in England. Edward's sympathies had long been on the side of
Balliol; border frays gave him an excuse for breaking the peace,
and he joined Balliol in besieging Berwick.)

The king of England, hearing that the Scots had
entered his land, and had done all the evils of which
we have spoken, although he himself had not yet
broken the peace and concord made between him
and David, son of lord Robert of Bruce, who had
married Edward's sister, who was with him in
Scotland, approached Berwick about the festival of

the apostles Philip and James (May 1.) in order to
vanquish the Scots and assist the king of Scotland,
having with him his own brother John of Eltham,
and many other noble earls, barons, knights, and
squires, and thirty thousand picked men, the king
of Scotland being then besieging that town. And
within the week after Ascension Day (May 20) the
two kings with their army made a vigorous assault
on the said town, but those within (on account
of the strength and height of the wall, which the
father of the king of England had caused to be
built when the town was in his power) bravely
resisted and manfully defended themselves, so that
the English could not force an entrance, although
they continued the siege. Then on the 14th of
the calends of August, to wit on the vigil of S.
Margaret, virgin and martyr (July 19), after breakfast,
came the Scots in great multitude to their destruction,
marching in three lines towards the town of Berwick,
against the two kings and their armies then besieging
it, who however were ready and informed of their
coming. But the Scots who marched in the first
line were so wounded in the face and blinded by
the multitude of the English arrows, in this battle
as in the previous one at Gledenmoor, that they
could not help themselves, and soon began to
turn their faces away from the blows of the arrows
and fall. Even after the English and the Scotch
alike were drawn up in triple line, the king
of Scotland being in the hindermost, the Scots
turned to meet and do battle with the line of him

who, not unjustly, was seeking his right to the kingdom. However, as it is said, their first line was soon thrown into confusion and overcome by his (Balliol's) army before the rest began to fight. And, while he scattered the first division, the other two wings fell in battle before the English. Those of the Scots who were behind took to flight on foot, but the English followed them on horseback down the the different lanes, and knocked down the wretched fugitives with staves with iron teeth. On that day were killed of the Scots, as was said, 7 earls, namely, those of Ross, of Lennox, of Carrick, of Sutherland, and three others, and 27 bannerets, and 36,320 foot soldiers, though, according to some, fewer, according to others, many more. Among others also fell lord Archibald of Douglas, who had been the chief cause of their coming to this destruction; had not night soon fallen, many more would have been killed.

Before the Scotch army had got as far as Berwick a monk, who was in their company and heard their deliberations, cried to them "Proceed no further! Let us all return; for I see Christ crucified coming against you in the air from Berwick with brandished spear." But they, like proud and obstinate men, confiding in their numbers, which were twice as great as the English, hardened their hearts and would not return. This was told by one of the Scots, who was made a knight just before the battle, and was captured in the battle and put to ransom, adding that two hundred and three Scots were made knights before the battle, and none of them

escaped death except himself and four only with
him.

(Berwick gave itself up to Edward; the national party in
Scotland seemed crushed; and the young David Bruce took
refuge in France.)

1334.—Of the homage done by Edward of Balliol.

Chronicle of Lanercost, p. 277.

On the nineteenth day of June, that is to say on the
feast of the holy martyrs, Gervasius and Prothasius, at
Newcastle-upon-Tyne, came the king of Scotland, and
the earls of Athol and Dunbar, Mar and Buchan; and
then in the presence of the two English earls—the
king's brothers, the earl of Cornwall and the earl of
Warrenne—and these four Scotch earls, and of the
archbishop of York and the bishops of Durham and
Carlisle, and an almost innumerable multitude of
clergy and people, the king of Scotland, Edward of
Balliol, did his homage to his lord Edward the third,
king of England, to hold the kingdom of Scotland
of him, as of his chief lord, and of his heirs and
successors for ever. And because the king of England
had assisted him to re-enter and take possession of
his kingdom of Scotland, from which he had been
expelled by the Scots for a time, and had incurred
great expenses, the king of Scotland yielded to him
five Scotch counties which are nearest to the English
March—namely, the counties of Berwick and Roxburgh, Peebles and Dumfries, and the town of Had-
ington and the town of Sedburgh, with its castle,
and the forests of Selkirk and Ettrick and Sedburgh,

so that all these should be separated from the crown of Scotland and annexed to the crown of England for ever. Thus there did not remain to the king of Scotland this side the Scotch sea,* more than five counties, to wit, Ayr, Dunbarton, Lanark, Stirling, and Wigtown in Galway beyond the Firth. All the above said were publicly confirmed by oath and writing and fit witnesses, and this being done the king returned to England.

1334.—Order against Oxford students seceding to Stamford.

Rymer, Fœdera, ii. 891.

(Owing to the frequent conflicts between Northerners and Southerners at Oxford, many students had withdrawn to Stamford, which seemed likely to become a formidable rival to Oxford and Cambridge.)

The king, to the sheriff of Lincoln, greeting. Whereas we are given to understand that many masters and scholars of our university of Oxford, under colour of certain dissensions lately, as it is said, arisen in that university, and with other idle pretexts, withdrawing themselves from that university, presume to betake themselves to the town of Stamford, and there carry on their studies and perform scholastic exercises, having by no means sought our assent or license ; which, if it were tolerated, would manifestly turn not only to our contempt and disgrace but also to the dispersion of our said university ;

* The Firth of Forth.

We, unwilling that schools or studies should in any wise be carried on elsewhere within our realm than in places where there are now universities, order and firmly enjoin you to go in person to the said town of Stamford, and there and elsewhere within your bailiwick where it is expedient, cause it to be publicly proclaimed with our authority, and prohibition made that any should carry on study or perform scholastic exercises elsewhere than in our said universities, under penalty of forfeiting to us all they can forfeit ; and cause us, without delay, to be informed distinctly and openly, in our chancery, and under your seal, of the names of those whom you find disobeying, after this proclamation and prohibition ;

For we will that speedy justice be done as is fitting to all and everyone ready to bring their complaints of any violence or injury done to them at the said city of Oxford, before our justices there, specially deputed for this purpose.

Witness the king at Windsor, the second day of August.

By the king and council.

(This vigorous measure was successful, but not until a writ had been issued next year ordering the seizure of the books of the disobedient.)

1334-6.—Unsuccessful expeditions of Edward into Scotland.

Murimuth, pp. 75-80.

(The cession of the Lothians by Balliol caused him to be again

driven out. The following is a short account of Edward's vain
endeavours to re-conquer Scotland for him.)

When the news came to the parliament that the
Scots had all revolted and had taken prisoner the
lord Richard Talbot and six other knights, and
had slain many foot-soldiers, the king declared that
he would go to Scotland to bridle the malice of
the Scots; and the people granted to him the
fifteenth penny of lay property, and from the cities
and burgesses the tenth penny, and the clergy
granted a tenth.

Also in the same parliament our lord the king
consented to go to the Holy Land at his own charge,
yet did not fix any certain time for beginning his
journey, but ordered that the archbishop of Canterbury should be sent to the pope and to the king
of France to agree about the time; in order that
the two kings with their forces, should set out at the
same time; but nothing was ever really done. . . .

Soon after Michaelmas the king marched to the
Scotch borders, and wintered in those parts; and
having heard that the earl of Athol had treacherously
joined the Scots, and that they were besieging the
lord Henry of Beaumont in a certain castle, he
entered Scotland and caused the siege to be raised;
and kept Christmas at Roxburgh. . . . . . .

The archbishop of Canterbury returned about
Epiphany (1335). . . . . And soon after Epiphany,
the king of France sent ambassadors to the king of
England, to wit the bishop of Avranches and a
certain baron, to bring about a peace with the

Scotch, and they waited in England till the middle
of Lent ; and then at Nottingham a truce was
granted until the feast of S. John the Baptist, in
order that the parliament might deal meanwhile with
these matters and others touching the state of the
realm.   In this parliament held at York, it was
ordained that the king and the earls and the barons
with their forces should enter Scotland and cross the
Scotch sea ; which soon afterwards was done.   But
the Scotch, unwilling to array battle in the open,
pretended that they wished peace ; and afterwards,
about Michaelmas, many made peace, especially the
earl of Athol ; but others refused ; so that soon after
the earl of Moray was captured at Edinburgh and
sent to be imprisoned in England, and the lord
Richard Talbot was redeemed for two thousand
marks.   But the earl of Athol, wishing to shew that
he had really joined the English, rode against the
Scots to besiege a castle and suddenly, having but a
small force with him, fell among the enemy who were
greatly superior in number; and willing not to yield but
to fight was slain with thirteen persons of less estate
after Michaelmas.   The king, however, still remained
on the Scotch borders and likewise also the ambassadors of the pope and the king of France, waiting
to bring about some peace or long truce, to us
useless.   .   .   .   This year the king had a tenth
from the burgesses, a fifteenth from his other
subjects, and a tenth from the clergy.   And about
Whitsuntide (1336) the king held a parliament at
Northampton, where he left the prelates and others

to treat, and he himself secretly rode towards Scotland, with very few followers, as far as Berwick; and thence taking a few troops he rode to the town of S. John (Perth), where he found his forces, who were surprised and wondered at his arrival. He caused that town to be fortified with ditches and walls, and sent his earls with the king of Scotland through the country, to see if they could join battle with the Scots; but none dared to await them, but lay in hiding in the mountains, marshes, and forests. . . . . In October died John of Eltham, earl of Cornwall, brother of the king of England, and this was in Scotland and not in battle. Also this year, our lord the king caused to be taken in every cathedral church all the money collected and placed there for the crusade. Also, this year, the pope recalled the tenth for six years which had been granted for the crusade, because the king of France put off his journey to the Holy Land too much, and the pope desired that what had been paid should be returned; but nothing was returned in England because the clergy granted it to the king.

1337.—Prohibition of the export of wool.

Murimuth, p. 81.

(This was probably intended partly to encourage the rising cloth manufacture in England, but partly also to coerce the earl of Flanders into joining Edward against Philip of Valois.)

The king summoned his parliament for the Monday after the feast of S. Matthew the apostle, and in this he made his eldest son, duke of Cornwall, the

lord Henry, son of the earl of Lancaster, earl of
Derby, the lord William of Bohun, earl of Northampton, the lord William of Montagu, earl of
Sarum, the lord Hugh of Audley, earl of Gloucester,
the lord William of Clinton, earl of Huntingdon,
the lord Robert of Ufford, earl of Suffolk. These
creations were made in the second Sunday in
Lent, at Westminster; where also he made 24
knights. Also in the same parliament it was
enacted that no wool growing in England should
leave the realm, but that cloth should be made
with it in England, and that all makers of cloth
should be welcomed in England wherever they
might come from, and that fit places should be
assigned to them and that they should have wages
from the king until they could make fitting gain
by their craft. Also it was enacted that no one
should use cloth made outside England and afterwards imported, except the king and queen and
their children. From which statutes no results
followed, nor did any one take the trouble to
observe them.

(Yet the Flemish weavers, who were entirely dependent upon
England for their wool, were thereby reduced to great distress.)

1329-1333.—How the lord sir Robert of Artois was chased out of the realm of France.

Froissart, ch. 25 (I. § 48). *Jehan le Bel*, ch. 19.

The man in the world that most aided king
Philip to attain to the crown of France was sir
Robert, earl of Artois, who was one of the sagest

and greatest lords in France, and come of high
lineage from the blood royal, and had to his wife
the sister of the said king Philip, and always was
his chief and special companion and lover in all his
estates.   And the space of three years all that was
done in the realm of France was done by his advice,
and without him nothing was done.   And, after, it
fortuned that this king Philip took a marvellous
great displeasure and hatred against this noble man,
sir Robert of Artois, for a plea that was moved
before   him   whereof   the   earl   of   Artois   was
cause.   For he would fain have won his intent by
virtue of a letter that he laid forth, the which was
not true as it was said.   Wherefore the king was in
such displeasure that if he had taken him in his ire
surely it had cost him his life, without remedy.   So
this sir Robert was fain to fly the realm of France,
and went to Namur to the earl John, his nephew.
Then the King took the earl's wife and her two
sons, who were his own nephews, John and Charles,
and did put them in prison.   And they were kept
straitly, and the king swear that they should never
come out of prison as long as they lived ; the king's
mind would be turned by no manner of means.

(Robert of Artois came to England probably in 1334, and in
1337 Edward gave him certain estates and a pension.)

1337.—How king Edward was counselled to make war against the French king.

Froissart, ch. 28 (1. § 56).   *Jehan le Bel*, ch. 25.

In this season when this crusade was in great

forwardness, for there was no speaking but thereof, sir Robert of Artois was as then in England, banished out of France, and was ever about king Edward ; and always he counselled him to defy the French king, who kept his heritages from him wrongfully; of which matter the king oftentimes counselled with them of his secret council, for gladly he would have had his right if he wist how. And also he thought that if he should demand his right and it were refused, what he might do then to amend it. For if he should then sit still and do not his devoir to recover his right, he should be more blamed than before ; yet he thought it were better to speak not thereof. For he saw well that by the puissance of his realm it would be hard for him to subdue the great realm of France without help from some other great lords, either of the empire or in other places, for his money. The king oftentimes desired counsel of his chief and special friends and counsellors. Finally, his counsellors answered him and said, "Sir, the matter is so weighty and of so high an enterprise that we dare not speak therein nor give you any counsel. But, sir, this we would counsel you to do: send sufficient messengers, well informed of your intention, to the earl of Hainault, whose daughter you have married, and to sir John of Hainault, his brother, who hath valiantly served you at all times. And desire them, by way of love, that they would counsel you in this matter, for they know better what pertaineth to such a matter than we do.

And, sir, if they agree to your intent, then will
they counsel you what friends you may best
make." The king was content with this answer,
and desired the bishop of Lincoln to take on him
this message, and with him two bannerets and two
doctors. They made them ready and took shipping
and arrived at Dunkirk, and rode through Flanders
till they came to Valenciennes, where they found the
earl lying in his bed sick of the gout, and with him
sir John his brother. They were greatly feasted,
and declared the cause of their coming, and showed
all the reasons and doubts that the king their master
had made. Then the earl said: "So help me God,
if the king's mind might be brought to pass, I would
be right glad thereof; for I had rather the wealth of
him that hath married my daughter, than of him that
never did nothing for me, though I have married his
sister. And also he did hinder the marriage of the
young duke of Brabant who should have married
one of my daughters. Wherefore I shall not fail
to aid my dear and well beloved son, the king of
England. I shall give him counsel and aid to the
best of my power, and so shall do John my brother
who hath served him ere this. Howbeit he must
have more help than ours, for Hainault is but a small
country in regard to the realm of France, and England
is far off to aid us." Then the bishop said, "Sir, we
thank you in our master's behalf, for the comfort that
you give us. Sir, we desire you to give our master
counsel what friends he were best to labour unto
to aid him." "Surely," said the earl, "I can not

devise a more puissant prince to aid him than the duke of Brabant who is his cousin germain. And also the bishop of Liège, the duke of Gueldres, who hath his sister to his wife, the archbishop of Cologne, the marquis of Juliers, sir Arnold of Blenkenheim, and the lord of Falkenberg. These lords are they that may make most men of war in a short space of any that I know. They are good men of war; they may well make ten thousand men of war so they have wages thereafter; they are people that would gladly win advantage. If it were so that the king, my son, your master, might get these lords to be on his part, and so to come into these parts, he might well go over the water of Oise and seek out king Philip to fight with him." With this answer these ambassadors returned into England to the king and reported all that they had done, whereof the king had great joy and was well comforted.*

1337.—To explain to the people the promises made to the king of France in order to preserve peace.

Rymer. Fœdera, 994.

(In this manifesto before beginning the war with France, Edward does not claim the French crown, and complains only of Philip's action in Guienne and Scotland.)

The king to the venerable father in Christ, John, archbishop of Canterbury, primate of all England, and to his trusty and well-beloved William of Clin-

---

* For Edward's claim to the French crown, see *Appendix*.

ton, earl of Huntingdon, who have been appointed to declare in the county of Kent certain things touching the defence of our realm, of holy church, and of our other lands, greeting;

We send you a certain schedule, herein enclosed, of the promises which we and our ambassadors have made to prevent war with the king of France;

Commanding you, and each of you, that you cause what is contained in that schedule to be clearly and fully explained to the clergy and people of that county, on the day and at the place mentioned in the commission which has been issued to you;

Persuading them, by all the ways and means you can, since that king threatens us with war, willing to consent neither to peace nor to negotiations for peace, whereby we are subjected to intolerable expense for public defence, to help us freely each of them, as far as their means permit; so acting in this, that we may have to justly commend your diligence.

Witness the king, at Westminster, the 28th day of August. By the king.

A similar order was sent to the following persons appointed in the following counties to make the same announcement—

(Then follows a list of persons so appointed, *e.g.*, in Oxfordshire and Bucks., the abbots of Abingdon and Osney and three knights.)

Schedule mentioned in the above order.

These are the offers made to the king of France by the king of England to prevent war.

In the first place, the king of England sent to the king of France divers solemn messages, praying him to restore the lands that he withheld from him, wilfully and against reason, in the duchy of Guienne; to none of which requests did the king of France consent; but at last he promised that, if the king of England would come to him in person, he would shew him justice, grace, and favour.

Trusting to this promise, the king of England passed privately into France and went to him, humbly requesting the return of those lands, offering and performing to the king what he was bound to do and more; but the king of France gave him words only and not deeds, and, moreover, while the negotiations were going on, encroached wrongfully more and more on the rights of the king of England in that duchy.

Also the king of England, seeing the ·harshness of the king of France, in order to have his good will and that which he wrongfully kept from him, made him the great offers below mentioned; that is to say, when one was refused he made him another;

First, the marriage of his eldest son, now duke of Cornwall, with the daughter of the king of France, without dowry;

Then, the marriage of his sister, now countess of Gueldres, with his son, with a very great sum of money;

Then, the marriage of his brother, the earl of

Cornwall, whom God assoil, with any lady of the blood royal of France ;

Then, to make redemption for disturbance, he offered him as much money as he could reasonably demand ;

Then, since the king of France gave the king of England to understand, that he wished to undertake a crusade to the Holy Land, and greatly desired to have the company of the king of England, and that he would do him grace and favour therefor, the king of England, in order that the prevention of the crusade might not be attributed to him, offered to the king of France to go in force with him on the crusade ; provided, however, that before going, he made full restitution to him of his lands;

Then, he offered to go with him on crusade, on condition that he made restitution of half or a certain part of his lands ;

Then, afterwards, he offered, with still greater liberality, to go with him on condition that, on his return from the Holy Land, he made full restitution.

Then, to stay the malice of the king of France, who tried to put upon the king of England the blame of preventing the crusade, he declared himself ready to undertake the crusade, on condition that, on his return, he did him justice.

But the king of France, who endeavoured in all ways that he could to injure the king of England and all his subjects, that he might keep what he unjustly withheld and conquer more from him, would

not accept any of these offers, but seeking occasion
to injure him, gave aid and maintenance to the
Scots, the enemies of the king of England, trying
to prevent him, by the Scotch war, from seeking
his rights elsewhere.

Also, then, from respect to the king of France
and at his request, the king of England granted
to the Scots a cessation of the war and a truce,
with hope of bringing about the peace;

But, during the truce, the Scots killed the earl
of Athol and others, and took many nobles faithful
to the king of England, and besieged and took
castles and other places from the king and his
subjects;

And, recently, at his request, he offered to the
Scots a truce for four or five years, on condition
that they restored what they had taken during the
former truce, in order that the crusade might take
place in the meantime;

To which restoration the king of France would
not consent, but supported the Scots in their malice
with all his power, and made open war without just
cause on the king of England, and sent to sea his
galleys and navy which he had prepared under
pretence of the crusade, with a great number of
armed men, to destroy the navy and subjects of the
king of England;

Which men have taken in war and spoiled many
ships of England and killed and taken the men who
were in them, and have landed in England and the
islands of the king of England, committing arson,

homicide, robberies, and other horrible crimes, according to their power.

Also then the king of England by the counsel and advice of the magnates and wise men of the realm, wishing to prevent the war if possible, sent solemn messages to the king of France, to offer him all he could without great disherison, to obtain peace ;

But the king of France, hardened in his malice, would not suffer these messages to be brought to him, nor consent to peace or negotiations for peace ; but sent a great and strong army to take into his hands by force the duchy before mentioned ; declaring, untruly, that the duchy was forfeited ;

Which army did great evils in the duchy, besieging and taking castles and towns as far as they could.

Also the king of France, to cover his malice, did try to misinform the pope and the other great men of Christendom with regard to the king of England ; aiming at conquering, as far he can, not only that duchy, but all the lands of the king of England.

These proposals and others the king of England and his council could think of, have been made to the king of France to secure peace, and if any man can find any other fitting way, he will be bound and ready to accept it.

1337.—How Jacques d'Artevelde governed all Flanders.

Froissart, ch. 29 (I. § 59). *Jehan le Bel*, ch. 25.

(The immediate cause of the rising in Ghent was the wool-famine, due to the count's hostility to England. The aristocratic canon of Liège, Jehan le Bel, is strongly prejudiced against the popular leader, and thus the following account is full of misrepresentation.)

In this season there was great discord between the earl of Flanders and the Flemings, for they would not obey him; and he durst not abide in Flanders but in great peril. And in the town of Ghent there was a man, a maker of honey, called Jacques d'Artevelde. He was entered into such fortune and grace of the people that all things were done that he did devise; he might command what he would through all Flanders, for there was no man, though he were never so great, that durst disobey his commandment. He had always going with him up and down in Ghent sixty or four score varlets armed, and among them there were three or four that knew the secrets of his mind. So that if he met a person that he hated or had in suspicion, immediately he was slain. For he had commanded his secret varlets that wheresoever he met any person and made such a sign to them, that immediately they should slay him whatsoever he were, without any words or reasoning. And by that means he made many to be slain, whereby he was so dreaded that none durst speak against anything that he willed to be done; so that every man was glad to make him good cheer. And these varlets when they had brought him home to his house, then they should go to dinner where they list; and after dinner return again into the street before his lodging, and there abide till he come out and to wait on him till supper time. These soldiers had each of them four Flemish groats by the day, and were paid truly weekly. Thus he had in every town soldiers and servants at his wages ready to do his commandment, and to espy if there were any person that would rebel against his mind, and to inform him thereof. And as soon as he knew any such he would never cease till they were banished or slain without respite. All such great men, as knights, squires, or burgesses of good towns, as he thought favourable to the earl in any manner, he banished them out of Flanders; and he would levy the moiety of their lands to his own use, and leave the other half to their wives and children. Such as were banished, of whom there were a great number, abode at Saint Omer. To speak properly, there was never in Flanders, nor in none other country, prince, duke, nor other, that ruled a country so peaceably, so long as this Jacques d'Artevelde did rule Flanders. He levied the rents, winages, and rights that pertained to the earl throughout all Flanders, and spent all at his pleasure without any account making. And when he would say that he lacked money they believed him, and so it behoved them to do, for none durst say against him. When he would borrow anything of any burgess, there was none durst say him nay.

Now the English Ambassadors kept an honourable estate at the town of Valenciennes. They thought it should be a great comfort to the king, their lord,

if they might get the Flemings to take their part.
Then they took counsel of the earl (of Hainault) in
that matter and he answered that truly it should be
one of the greatest aids that they could have. But he
said he thought their labour could not prevail without
they get first the goodwill of Jacques d'Artevelde.
Then they said they would essay what they could do ;
and so, thereupon, they departed from Valenciennes
and went into Flanders, and departed into three
or four companies. Some went to Bruges, some
to Ypres, and some to Ghent. And all kept such
state and spent so much that it seemed that silver
and gold fell out of their hands; and they made many
great promises and offers to them that they spake
to for that matter. And the bishop, with a certain
man with him, went to Ghent, and he did so much,
what with fair words and otherwise, that he got
the accord of Jaques d'Artevelde. And he got
great grace in the town, and specially of an old
knight that dwelt in Ghent, who was there right
well beloved, called the lord of Courtraisen, a
knight banneret, reputed for a hardy knight, who
had always served truly his lords. This knight
did much honour to the Englishmen, as a valiant
knight ought to do to all strangers. Of this he
was accused to the French king, who immediately
sent a strait commandment to the earl of Flanders
that he should send for this said knight, and as
soon as he had him to strike off his head. The
earl, who durst not break the King's commandment, did so much that this knight came to him

at his sending as one that thought no evil, and at
once he was taken and his head struck off; whereof
many folks were sorry and were sore displeased with
the Count, for he was well beloved with the lords
of the country.   These English lords did so much
that Jacques d'Artevelde divers times had together
the councils of the good towns to speak of the
business that these lords of England desired, and
of the franchises and amities that they offered them
in the king of England's behalf.   So often they
spake of this matter, that finally they agreed that
the king of England might come and go into
Flanders at his pleasure.   Howbeit, they said they
were so sore bound to the French king that they
might not enter into the realm of France to make
any war.

1337, Nov. 11.—Of the battle of Cadsand between the Englishmen and the Frenchmen.

Froissart, ch. 30-1 (1. § 63).

(Although no formal declaration of war between Edward and
Philip of Valois had yet been made, the French fleet attacked
Portsmouth, and the English attacked Cadsand.)

In this season there were in the isle of Cadsand
certain knights and squires of Flanders in garrison.
.   .   .   They kept that passage against the Englishmen and made covert war.   And when Edward heard
of the garrison of Cadsand, he said he would provide
for them shortly.   And anon after, he ordained the
earl of Derby, sir Walter Manny, and divers other
knights and squires with five hundred men of arms

and two thousand archers, and they took shipping
at London in the river Thames. The first tide
they went to Gravesend, the next day to Margate,
and at the third tide they took the sea and sailed
into Flanders. So they apparelled themselves and
came near to Cadsand.

When the Englishmen saw the town of Cadsand
before them, they made them ready, and had wind
and tide to serve them. And so in the name of
God and Saint George they approached, and blew
up their trumpets, and set their archers before them,
and sailed toward the town. They of Cadsand saw
well this great ship approach. They knew well
they were Englishmen, and arranged themselves on
the dykes and on the sands with their banners before
them; and they made sixteen new knights. They
were five thousand men of war, good knights and
squires. There was sir Guy of Flanders, a good
and a sure knight, but he was a bastard, and he
desired all his company to do well their devoir.
The Englishmen were desirous to assail and the
Flemings to defend. The English archers began
to shout and cried their cries, so that such as kept
the passage were fain perforce to recoil back. At
this first assault there were divers sore hurt, and
the Englishmen took land and came and fought
hand to hand. The Flemings fought valiantly to
defend the passage, and the Englishmen assaulted
chivalrously. The earl of Derby was that day a
good knight; and at the first assault he was so
forward that he was striken to the earth. And then

the lord of Manny did him great comfort, for by pure feat of arms he raised him up again and brought him out of peril, and cried, " Lancaster! for the earl of Derby!" Then they approached on every part and many were hurt, but more of the Flemings than the Englishmen, for the archers shot so wholly together that they did the Flemings much damage. Thus in the haven of Cadsand there was a sore battle; for the Flemings were good men of war, chosen out by the earl of Flanders to defend that passage against the Englishmen. . . . .

There was a sore battle and well fought, hand to hand, but finally the Flemings were put to the chase and were slain more than three thousand, what in the haven, streets, and houses. Sir Guy, the bastard of Flanders, was taken, and sir Dutres of Hallwyn and sir John of Rhodes were slain, and the two brethren of Bonquedent, and sir Giles de L'Etriefe, and more than twenty-six knights and squires. And the town was taken, pillaged, and all the goods and prisoners put into the ships and the town burnt. And so thus the Englishmen returned into England without any damage. The King caused sir Guy, bastard of Flanders, to swear and to bind himself prisoner. And in the same year he became English, and did faith and homage to the King of England.

1338.—How Black Agnes defended Dunbar.

Chronicle of Lanercost, 295-298.

(The siege of Dunbar was the last great effort of Edward

in Scotland; after five months it had to be abandoned, and Edward henceforth directed his efforts chiefly against France).

The king sent the lord William of Montague, earl of Salisbury, the earl of Gloucester, the earl of Derby, three barons, Percy, Neville, and Stafford, and the earl of Riddesdale, with twenty thousand men, into Scotland, to join the Scotch king (Balliol), ordering them vigorously to besiege the castle of Dunbar, which annoyed and troubled the whole land of Lothian. So the castle was besieged without intermission, and those within were surrounded with a deep ditch that they should not escape, and wooden houses were made in front of the gate, and tents were erected in which the more noble of the army dwelt. . . . . . But the castle defended itself manfully; for the countess of March, who was the chief warden of the castle, was the sister of the earl of Moray, who had been taken prisoner in Scotland and taken to England to the castle of Nottingham and there imprisoned. . . . . . After Easter, this earl was taken back to Scotland to Dunbar, to see if the countess, his sister, would give up the castle to save his life; but she replied that it was her lord's castle and given her to guard, nor would she yield it to any save at his command; and when those who were besieging her said that then her brother should die, she replied, " If you do that, then I shall be heir of the earldom of Moray," for her brother had no children. However, the English did not like to do what they had threatened, but preferred to take him back to Eng-

land and keep him in prison, as before. . . . .
And then because the king wished to cross the sea,
the lord William of Montague and the other earls
who were with him at the siege of Dunbar, unwilling
that he should go to any peril without them, gave
truce to those who were in the castle, on condition
that during the truce no change should be made
around or within the castle, or in the houses that
the English had made outside, although this could
not afterwards be observed.

(The Scotch rhyming chronicler, Andrew of Wyntown, tells
how Montague had made

> "a mickel and right stalwart engine,"
> and "warped * at the walls great stones,"
> but all in vain,
> " And also when they casten had,
> With a towel a damosel
> Arrayëd jolily † and well
> Wipëd the wall that they might see
> To make them more annoyed be." ll. 4859, sqq.)

1338.—How Edward crossed the sea and was made Vicar of the Empire.

Knighton, 2571-2.

Then was made a truce between England and
Scotland to last for one year, and the siege of
Dunbar was raised.   King Edward meanwhile sent
beyond sea the lord William Bohun, earl of Northampton, and the lord Geoffrey Scrope the chief
justice of England and many others who landed at
Antwerp in Brabant. On the day of the Translation

----

* Threw.   † Prettily.

of S. Thomas, when all had been arranged and provided for the passage, the king put to sea with a great force, having with him the earls and magnates of the realm, such as the earls of Derby, of Salisbury, and Norfolk, and many nobles with them, and a great multitude of archers and Welsh : and he landed at Antwerp to join his wife and sons, on the feast of S. Kenelm. The Flemings rejoiced at his arrival and promised their aid : for he had given them satisfaction in the matter of certain ships that the English had taken from them and destroyed. . . . . . And when the king had come into those parts he found none in whom he could trust, so that he told the bishop of Lincoln and his other councillors that he had been ill advised. With headstrong course he pursued his way for eight days to Cologne to the duke of Bavaria, who had made himself emperor and dwelt in High Germany.* When the emperor heard of the coming of king Edward, he came to meet him, journeying for four days to a certain town of the name of Coblenz, and there he received the king with great honour. One chair was prepared for the emperor, one for the king, richly decked in the market place out-of-doors ; there sat the emperor and king Edward beside him ; and there were with them four dukes, three archbishops, and six bishops, and thirty-seven earls, and of barons, bannerets, knights, and other comers according to the reckoning of the heralds seventeen thousand. The emperor held in his right hand the imperial sceptre, and in his left

* See *Appendix.*

hand a round gold ball, which signifies the rule of the whole world; while over his head a knight held an unsheathed sword. There in the presence of the assembled people the emperor declared the unnaturalness, disobedience, and depravity that the king of France had shewn towards him; defied the king of France; and declared him and all his adherents under forfeiture. Then the emperor made king Edward his vicar, and gave him full power in his stead from Cologne to the sea; and in addition gave him a charter in the sight of all the people. On the morrow there came together at the mother-church the emperor and the king of England with the rest of the magnates and the archbishops, and they celebrated mass, and immediately after mass both the emperor and all the other magnates swore that they would help and support him against the king of France, to live and to die, for the next seven years following, supposing that war between the said kings should last so long. And likewise they all swore to the king of England that all the princes from Cologne to the sea would speedily join the king of England, and be always ready to march at any time that they were summoned, against the king of France, either in his company or when he should appoint. And if it should happen that any of them did not obey the king of England in the foregoing, all the other princes of high Germany would rise against him and destroy him. These treaties having been made, the king took leave of the emperor and returned to Brabant.

1339.—How the king of England and the French king appointed a day to fight together.

Froissart, ch. 40-2 (1. §§ 84-88).

(The greater part of the year was occupied with negotiations with the German princes and with the pope, who urged Edward to dissolve his alliance with the excommunicated emperor, Louis of Bavaria. In the autumn, the king brought together his allies, and made his first attempt on France, crossing the Oise, and meeting the French army near S. Quentin.)

Thus these two kings were lodged between Buiron-fosse and Flamengery in the plain fields without any advantage. I think there was never seen before so goodly an assembly of noble men together, as was there. When the king of England, being in the chapel of Tierache, knew how that king Philip was within two leagues, then he called the lords of his host together, and demanded of them what he should do, his honour saved, for he said that his intention was to give battle. Then the lords beheld each other, and they desired the duke of Brabant to show first his intent; the duke said, that he agreed that they should give battle, for otherwise, he said, they could not depart saving their honours; wherefore he counselled that they should send heralds to the French king to demand a day of battle. Then a herald of the duke of Gueldres, who knew well the language of French, was informed what he should say and so he rode till he came into the French host; and then he drew him to king Philip and to his council, and said: "Sir, the king of England is in the field and desireth to have battle, power against power"; the which thing king Philip granted and took the day, the Friday next after; and then it was Wednesday. And so the herald returned, well rewarded with good furred gowns given him by the French king and other lords because of the tidings that he brought. So thus the day was agreed upon, and knowledge was made thereof to all the lords of both the hosts, and so every man made him ready to the matter. The Thursday in the morning there were two knights of the earl of Hainault's, the lord Faguinelles and the lord of Tupeney, they mounted on their horses, and they two all alone departed from the French host, and rode to view the English host; so they rode coasting the host, and it fortuned that the lord of Faguinelles' horse took the bridle in the teeth in such wise that his master could not rule him; and so, whether he would or not, the horse brought him into the English host, and there he fell in the hands of the Germans, who perceived well that he was none of their company, and set on him, and took him and his horse; and so he was prisoner to five or six gentlemen of Germany; and anon they set him to his ransom. And when they understood that he was a Hainaulter, they demanded of him if he knew sir John of Hainault, and he answered "Yes" and desired them for the love of God to bring him to his presence, for he knew well that he would pay his ransom for him; thereof were the Germans joyous, and so brought him to the lord Beaumont, who immediately did pledge him out from his masters' hands; and the lord of Faguinelles returned again to the earl of Hainault, and he had his horse again delivered to him at the request of the lord Beaumont. Thus passed that day, and none other thing done that ought to be remembered.

When the Friday came, in the morning both hosts apparelled themselves ready, and every lord heard mass among their own companies, and divers were shriven. . . . . . It might well be marvelled, how so goodly a sight of men of war so near together should depart without battle. But the Frenchmen were not all of one accord; they were of divers opinions; some said it were a great shame an they fought not, seeing their enemies so near them in their own country, ranged in the field, and also had promised to fight with them; and some other said it should be a great folly to fight, for it was hard to know every man's mind, and jeopardy of treason: for, they said, if fortune were contrary to their king, as to lose the field, he then should put his whole realm in a jeopardy to be lost; and even if he did discomfort his enemies, yet, for all that, he should be never the nearer of the realm of England, nor of such lands pertaining to any of those lords that be with him allied. Thus in striving of divers opinions the day passed, till it was past noon; and then suddenly there started a hare among the Frenchmen; and such as saw her cried and made great noise, whereby such as were behind thought they before had been fighting, and so put on their helms and took their spears in their hands, and so there were made

divers new knights, and especially the earl of Hainault
made thirteen, who were ever after called knights of
the hare.   Thus that battle stood still all that Friday;
and besides this strife between the councillors of
France, there were brought in letters to the host of
recommendation to the French king and to his
council from king Robert of Sicily, the which king,
as it was said, was a great astronomer, and full of
great science.   He had often times sought his books
on the estate of the kings of England and of France,
and he found by his astrology and by the influence
of the heavens, that if the French king ever fought
with king Edward of England, he should be discom-
forted; wherefore he, like a king of great wisdom
and as he that doubted the peril of the French king
his cousin, sent often times letters to king Philip and
to his council, that in no wise he should make any
battle against the Englishmen, where king Edward
was personally present.   So that, what with doubt
and with such writing from the king of Sicily, divers
of the great lords of France were sore abashed; and
also king Philip was informed thereof.   Howbeit,
yet he had great will to give battle; but he was so
counselled to the contrary, that the day passed without battle and every man withdrew to their lodgings.
And when the earl of Hainault saw that they would
not fight he departed with all his whole company,
and went back the same night to Quesnoy.   And
the king of England, the duke of Brabant, and all
the other lords retired, and trussed all their baggages
and went the same night to Davesnes, in Hainault.

And the next day they took leave each of other ; and the Germans and the Brabanters departed, and the king went into Brabant with the duke his cousin.

1340, Jan.—How king Edward took on him to bear the arms of France, and the name to be called king thereof.

Froissart, ch. 43 (1. §§ 88-90). *Jehan le Bel*, ch. 33.

Then the king of England was sore desired of all his allies in the empire that he should require them of Flanders to aid and to maintain his war, and to defy the French king, and to go with him where he would have them ; and that, on their so doing, he should promise them to recover Lille, Douay, and Bethune.* This request was well heard of the Flemings, and thereupon they desired to take counsel among themselves. And so they took counsel at good leisure, and then they said to the king, "Sir, ere this time ye have made to us request in this behalf. Sir, if we might well do this, saving your honour, and to save ourselves, we would gladly do it. But, sir, we be bound by faith and oath, and on the sum of two million florins in the pope's chamber, that we may make or move no war against the king of France, on pain to lose the said sum and beside that to run in danger of the sentence of cursing. But, sir, if you will take on you the arms of France and quarter them with the arms of England, and call yourself king

* Yielded to the king of France by the "Iniquitous Treaty" of 1305.

of France, as you ought to be of right, then we will take you for rightful king of France and demand of you quittance of our bonds; and so you will give us pardon thereof, as king of France. By this means we shall be assured and acquitted withal, and so then we will go with you whithersoever you will have us." Then the king took counsel, for he thought it was a sore matter to take on him the arms of France and the name, while, as then, he had conquered nothing thereof, nor could not tell what should fall thereof nor whether he should conquer it or not. And, on the other side, loth he was to refuse the comfort and aid of the Flemings, who might do him more aid than any other. So the king took counsel of the lords of the empire and of the lord Robert of Artois, and with other of his special friends, and so that finally, the good and the evil weighed, he answered to the Flemings, that if they would swear and seal to this agreement, and promise to maintain his war, he would do all this with a good will, and promised to get them again Lille, Douay, and Bethune. And they all answered that they were content. Then there was a day assigned to meet at Ghent, at the which day the King was there, and the most part of the said lords, and all the councils generally in Flanders. And so then all these said matters were rehearsed, sworn, and sealed; and the king quartered the arms of France with England, and from thenceforth took on him the name of the king of France and so continued till he left it again by composition.

Thus every man departed and went home. The king of England went to Antwerp, and the queen abode still at Ghent, and was oftentimes visited by Jacques d'Artevelde and by other lords, ladies, and damsels of Ghent.

(Next month Edward returned to England.)

1339.—At a College Meeting.

Rogers, History of Agriculture, ii. 672.

(At Merton College, Oxford, the warden and fellows were bound to meet three times a year at a "scrutiny," wherein each gave his opinion on the condition of the college. Of three of these meetings some rough notes, taken by one who was present, have been preserved.)

Middleton.—William the chaplain has often insulted the fellows.

Handel.—It would be well if the senior fellows were summoned to make peace between Wylie and Finmer.

Westcombe.—The noise the fellows make in their rooms.

Humberstone. — The quarrel between Wylie and Finmer. The fellows keep dogs, and progress in their studies is prevented by idleness. The statute is not observed, for we have no bursars. Also it would be well if the land in Little Wolford were let to a farmer.

Finmer.—Wylie, although appointed under the statute to audit accounts, will not audit them, and though thrice summoned and again called upon by the fellows, has rebelliously refused, and so falls under the statute ; and he unjustly receives better commons, and they who ought to proceed against him are too remiss.

Wanting.—The warden should not go on insulting the senior fellows in the way he has begun.

Wylie.—Somebody should be sent to Stratton to enquire about the college estates and other business.

Lynham.—As to allaying the quarrels among the fellows.

Sutton.—They ought to have a keeper of pledges,* but have not, and there is a deficit ; and it is said that some books are sold, without the college or the fellows benefiting by it. The warden does not enforce process against the debtors of the college and especially against the bailiff of Elham ; and Wanting owes the bailiff of Elham seven pounds and sixteen pence which belong to the college, and as he excuses himself from all other business, he ought not to take a part in these college meetings. . . . .

Handel would be glad if a volume of decrees and of decretals were placed in the library and if the books of the college were arranged. .

Buckingham.—Wanting has sold the college horses at Elham, and has kept the money in his hands, and has rendered no account nor has the bailiff. . . . There should not be a number of people taking notes in the meeting.

* Deposited with the college by students to whom loans had been made.

Dumbleton.—Nothing.

Monby.—Wylie has publicly, in the presence of all the fellows, insulted Finmer.

Leverington.—The seneschal is not present in chapel on saints' days, but is absent for the most part.

. . . .

Wylie begs that what has been said by Elyndon and Wanting be corrected, and recommends charity. The warden should correct it, especially what had been said to the warden in the meeting, and above all what Elyndon said, that the reputations of some of the fellows were tarnished ; and how that Durant accused Wylie of planning with the other seniors to prevent the election of a fellow, and that he had this from those who were recently in London.

Middleton.—Elham is in fault as to the breaking of the hall door. We ought to have a mill at Seaton.

Handel.— This opportunity should be taken of restoring peace. The juniors should show reverence to the seniors, and everyone should be enjoined publicly to observe charity, and each should try to bring this about as far as he can.

Humberstone.—The warden ought by statute to get the help of some of the fellows who are impartial to put an end to the quarrel between Wylie and Finmer. Wanting has behaved disrespectfully towards the warden by publicly addressing him as Robert.

1340.—A Lesson on Usury.

Ayenbite of Inwyt (Remorse of Conscience), ed. Early English Text Society, p. 35.

(The two following extracts are most valuable illustrations of the teaching of the pulpit and confessional. The *direct* payment of interest was illegal.)

There are seven kinds of usury. The first is lending that lendeth silver for other things, where over and above the capital sum the lender taketh the profits either in pence, or in horses, or in corn, or in wine, or in fruits of the ground that he taketh in mortgage, without reckoning these profits as part-payment. And what is worse, he will reckon twice, or even thrice in the year in order to raise the rate of usury, and yet he hath gifts as well for each term; and he maketh often of the usury a principal debt. These are usuries evil and foul. The courteous lender is he that lendeth without always making bargains for profit, either in pence, or in horses, or in cups of gold, or in silver, or in robes, or in tuns of wine, or in fat swine, or in services of horses or carts, or providings for himself or his children, or in any other things that he takes by reason of the loan. This is the first manner of usury, that is, lending wickedly. The other manner of usury is in those that do not themselves lend, but that which their fathers or the fathers of their wives or their elders have received in pledge and

they inherit, by usury they retain and will not yield
it up. The third manner of usury is in them that
have shame to lend with their own hand, but they
lend their pence through their servants or other
men. These are the master money-lenders. Of
such sin great men are not quit, who hold and
sustain Jews and usurers that lend and destroy the
country; and the great men take the rewards and
the great gifts, and oftentimes the ransom-money
of the goods of the poor. The fourth manner is
in those that lend with other men's silver that they
buy at small cost in order to lend at a greater.
These are the little usurers that teach so much
foul craft. The fifth manner is in bargaining when
men sell a thing, whatsoever it is, for more than
it is worth at the time. And what is worse, is
wickedly selling at that time when they see their
wares are most needed; then they sell the thing
for twice the dearer, or thrice as much as the thing
is worth. Such folk do much evil. For their
bargaining destroyeth and maketh beggars of knights
and nobles that follow tournaments. And they take
their lands and their heritage in pledge and mortgage, from which they never acquit them. Others
sin in buying things, as corn, or wine, or other
things, for less than half the pence that it is worth,
and then they sell them again for twice as
much, or thrice the dearer. Others buy things
when they are least worth and of great cheapness,
as corn sold in harvest time, or wine, or bargains,
in order to sell them again whenever they are most

dear. And they wish for a dear time in order to sell the dearer. Others buy corn in the blade and vines in the flower, when they are of fair-shewing and good forwardness, that they may have, whatever befal, their wealth safe. The sixth manner is when they give their pence to merchants in such wise that they are fellows in winning but not in losing. . . . . . The seventh manner is in those that lend their poor neighbours, in their needs, a little silver, or corn, or do them a little courtesy. And when they see them poor and needy, then they make with them a bargain to do their work, and for the pence they have before given to the poor man or the corn they have lent him, they have three pennyworth of work for one penny.

1340.—A Lesson on Trade.

Ayenbite of Inwyt, ed. E.E.T.S., p. 44.

The eighth bough of Avarice is chaffering, wherein one sinneth in many ways, for worldly winning; and, namely, in seven manners. The first is to sell the things as dear as one may, and to buy as good cheap as one may. The next is lying, swearing, and forswearing, the higher to sell their wares. The third manner is by weights and measures, and that may be in three ways. The first when one hath divers weights or divers measures, and buyeth by the greatest weights or the greatest measures and selleth by the least. The other manner is when one hath rightful weights and rightful measures to sell untruly, as do the taverners that fill the measure with scum. The third manner is when those that sell by weight contrive that the thing that they weigh showeth more heavy. The fourth manner to sin in chaffering is to sell to time. Of this we have spoken above. The fifth manner is to sell otherwise than one hath showed before; as doth these scriveners that showeth good letter at beginning and after do badly. The sixth is to hide the truth about the thing that one will sell; as do the dealers of horses. The seventh is to contrive that the thing one selleth maketh for to show better than it is; as do the sellers of cloth that choose dim places wherein to sell their cloth. In many other manners one may sin in chafferings, but long thing it were to say.

1340.—Here beginneth the statute made at Westminster in the 14th year of king Edward the third.

Public General Acts, Anno xiv. Ed. III.

(In order to obtain supplies for the war, Edward gave his assent to several reforming statutes, of which the following is the most important. It is a clearer declaration than any previously made of the principle that no taxation should be imposed except by the consent of parliament.)

Edward by the grace of God, etc., to all them etc., greeting. Know ye that whereas the prelates, earls, barons, and commons of the realm of England, in our present parliament holden at Westminster, the Wednesday next after the Sunday of middle Lent, the 14th year of our reign of England and the first of France, have granted to us of their good grace

and good will, in aid of the speed of our great
business which we have to do as well on this side
the sea as beyond, the 9th sheaf, the 9th fleece, and
the 9th lamb to be taken by two years next coming
. . . . and the citizens and burgesses of boroughs
the true 9th part of all their goods, and merchants
who dwell not in cities and boroughs as well as
others who dwell in forests and wastes and live not
of gain nor of store of sheep, the 15th of their goods
lawfully to the value; we, willing to provide to the
indemnity of the said prelates, earls, barons, and
other of the commonalty, and also of the citizens,
burgesses, and merchants aforesaid, will and grant
for us and our heirs to the same prelates, earls,
barons, and commons, citizens, burgesses, and
merchants that the same grant which is so chargeable
shall not another time be had forth in example nor
fall to their prejudice in time to come, nor that they
be from henceforth charged nor grieved to make any
aid or to sustain charge, if it be not by the common
assent of the prelates, earls, barons, and other great
men and commons of the said realm of England and
that in the parliament.   And that all the profits
rising of the said aid, and of wards and marriages,
customs and escheats, and other profits rising of the
said realm of England shall be set and dispended
upon the maintenance of the safeguard of our said
realm of England and of our wars of Scotland,
France, and Gascony, and in no place elsewhere
during the said wars.*

* For taxation under Edward the third, see *Appendix.*

1340, June 24.—Of the battle on the sea before Sluys in Flanders between the king of England and the Frenchmen.

Froissart, ch. 50 (I. § 114).

On midsummer even in the year of our Lord 1340, all the English fleet was departed out of the river of Thames, and took the way to Sluys. And the same time, between Blankenberg and Sluys on the sea, was sir Hugh Kiriel, sir Peter Bahucet, and Barbenoir, and more than sixscore great vessels besides others; and they were of Normans, Genoese, and Picards, about the number of forty thousand. There they were laid by the French king to bar the king of England's passage. The king of England and his men came sailing till they came before Sluys. And when the king saw so great a number of ships that their masts seemed to be like a great wood, he demanded of the master of his ship what people he thought they were. He answered and said, "Sir, I think they are Normans, laid here by the French king, and they have done great displeasure in England, burnt your town of Southampton and taken your great ship, the Christopher." "Ah!" quoth the king, "I have long desired to fight with the Frenchmen, and now shall I fight with some of them, by the grace of God and Saint George; for truly they have done me so many displeasures that I will be revenged, and I may." Then the king set all his ships in order, the greatest before, well furnished with archers, and ever between two ships of archers he had one ship with men of

arms.   Then he made another line to lie aloof
with archers to comfort ever them that were most
weary if need were.   And there were a great number
of countesses, ladies, knights' wives, and other
damosels, that were going to see the queen at Ghent;
these ladies the king caused to be well kept with
three hundred men at arms and five hundred archers.
When the king and his marshals had ordered his
lines of battle, he drew up the sails and came with
a quarter wind to have the advantage of the sun.
And so, at last, they turned a little to get the wind
at will; and when the Normans saw them recoil
back they had marvel why they did so.   And some
said, "They think themselves not meet to meddle
with us, wherefore they will go back."   They saw
well how the king of England was there personally,
by reasons of his banners.   Then they did put their
fleet in order, for they were sage and good men
of war on the sea; and did set the Christopher,
the which they had won the year before, to be
foremost, with many trumpets and instruments, and
so set on their enemies.   There began a sore battle
on both parts; archers and crossbows began to shoot;
men of arms approached and fought hand to hand;
and the better to come together they had great
hooks and grappling irons to cast out of one ship
into another, and so tied them fast together.   There
were many deeds of arms done, taking and rescuing
again.   And at last the great Christopher was first
won by the Englishmen, and all that were within
it taken or slain.   Then there was great noise and

cry, and the Englishmen approached and fortified
the Christopher with archers, and made it to pass
on before to fight with the Genoese. This battle
was right fierce and terrible, for the battles on the
sea are more dangerous and fiercer than the battles
by land; for on the sea there is no recoiling nor
fleeing, there is no remedy but to fight and to abide
fortune and every man to shew his prowess. Of a
truth sir Hugh Kiriel and sir Bahucet and Barbenoir
were right good and expert men of war. This
battle lasted from the morning till it was noon and
the Englishmen endured much pain, for their enemies
were four against one and all good men on the
sea. There the king of England was a noble knight
of his own hands; he was in the flower of his youth.
In likewise so were the earls of Derby, Pembroke,
Hereford, Huntingdon, Northampton, and Gloucester, sir Reynold Cobham, sir Richard Stafford, the lord
Percy, sir Walter of Manny, sir Henry of Flanders, sir
John Chandos, sir Robert of Artois, called the earl of
Richmond, and divers other lords and knights who
bore themselves so valiantly, with some succours that
they had of Bruges and of the country there about, that
they obtained the victory. So that the Frenchmen,
Normans, and others were discomfitted, slain, and
drowned; there was not one that escaped, but all
were slain. When this victory was achieved, the
king all that night abode in his ship before Sluys
with great noise of trumpets and other instruments.
Thither came to see the king divers of Flanders,
such as heard of the king's coming. And then

the king demanded of the burgesses of Bruges how Jacques d'Artevelde did. They answered that he was gone to the earl of Hainault against the duke of Normandy with sixty thousand Flemings. And the next day, the which was midsummer day, the king and all his took land. And the king, on foot, went a pilgrimage to our lady of Ardenburg and there heard mass and dined; and then took his horse and rode to Ghent, where the queen received him with great joy; and all his baggage came after, little by little. Then the king wrote to the count of Hainault and to them within the castle of Thun*, certifying them of his arrival. And when the count knew thereof, and that the king had discomfited the army on the sea, he dislodged, and gave leave to all the soldiers to depart. And he took with him to Valenciennes all the great lords and there feasted them honourably, and especially the duke of Brabant and Jacques d'Artevelde. And there Jacques d'Artevelde, openly in the market place, in the presence of all the lords and of all such as would hear him, declared what right the king of England had to the crown of France, and also how puissant the three countries were of Flanders, Hainault, and Brabant, surely joined in one alliance. And he did so by his great wisdom and pleasant words that all people that heard him praised him much, and said how he had nobly spoken and by great experience. And thus he was greatly praised and it was said that he was well

* Which had been besieged by the French.

worthy to govern the county of Flanders. Then
the lords departed and promised to meet again
within eight days at Ghent, to see the king of
England, and so they did. And the king feasted
them honourably, and so did the queen, who was
as then newly delivered of a son called John, who
afterwards became duke of Lancaster by his marriage
to the daughter of duke Henry of Lancaster.

1340.—How the king of England besieged the city of Tournay with great puissance.

Froissart, ch. 53, 54, 56, 57, 63.

When the time approached that the king and his
allies should meet before Tournay, and that the corn
began to ripen, he departed from Ghent with seven
earls of his country, eight prelates, thirty-eight
baronets, two hundred knights, four thousand men at
arms, and nine thousand archers, beside footmen.
All his host passed through the town of Oudenarde,
and so passed the river Scheldt, and lodged before
Tournay at the gate called St. Martin, the way
towards Lisle and Douai. Then anon after came the
duke of Brabant with more than twenty thousand
men, knights, squires, and commoners, and he lodged
at the bridge of Ayres by the river Scheldt between
the abbey of St. Nicholas and the gate Valentinois.
Next to him came the earl of Hainault with a goodly
company of his country, with many of Holland and
Zealand, and he was lodged between the king and
the duke of Brabant. Then came Jacques d'Artevelde
with more than sixty thousand Flemings, beside them

of Ypres, Poperingue, Cassel, Bruges. Jacques
d'Artevelde lodged at the gate of St. Fountain. The
duke of Gueldres, the earl of Juliers, and all the
Germans were lodged on the other side towards
Hainault. Thus the city of Tournay was environed
round about, and every host might resort each to the
other, so that none could issue without spying. The
siege enduring, they without were well provided with
victuals and at a proper price; for it came to them
from all parts.

Also the Flemings oftentimes assailed them of
Tournay, and had made ships, belfries, and instruments of assault; so that every day lightly there was
skirmishing and divers hurt of one and other. The
Flemings took much pain to trouble them of Tournay;
among other assaults there was one endured a whole
day; there were many feats of arms done, for all the
lords and knights that were at Tournay were thereat;
for the assault was made in ships and vessels wrought
with intent to break the barriers and the postern of
the arch; but it was so well defended that the
Flemings won nothing; there they lost a ship with
some six score men, the which were drowned, and at
night they withdrew sore troubled. . . . .
And because the victuals within the city began to
minish, the French lords within caused to leave the
town all manner of poor people, such as were not
furnished to abide the adventure of the siege; they
were put out in the open day, and they passed
through the duke of Brabant's host, who showed
their grief; for he caused them to be safely brought

to the French host at Arras, where the king lay ; and there he made a great assembly of men of his own country and part out of the empire. Thither came to him the king of Bohemia, the duke of Lorraine, the earl of Bar, the bishops of Metz and Verdun, the earl of Montbeliard, sir John of Chalons, the earl of Geneva, the earl of Savoy, and the lord Lewis of Savoy his brother. All these lords came to serve the French king with all their powers. Also thither came the duke of Brittany, the duke of Burgundy, the duke of Bourbon, the earl of Alençon, the earl of Flanders, the earl of Forêt, the earl of Armagnac, the earl of Blois, sir Charles of Blois, the earl of Harcourt, the earl of Dammartin, the lord Coucy, and divers other lords and knights. And after came the king of Navarre with a goodly number of men of war out of the country in France that he held of the French king. Also there was the king of Scots with a certain number appointed to him.

When all these said lords were come to Arras to the French king, then he removed and came to a little river three leagues from Tournay ; the water was deep, and round about full of marshes, so that no man could pass but by a little way, so narrow that two horses could not pass abreast ; there the king lay, and passed not the river, for he durst not. The next day the hosts lay still ; some of the lords counselled to make bridges to pass over the water at their case ; then there were men sent to view the passage, and when they had well viewed everything, they thought it was but a lost labour, and they showed

6

the king how that there was no passage but at the bridge of Tressin. Thus the matter abode in the same case. The tidings anon spread abroad how the French king was lodged between the bridge of Tressin and the bridge of Bouvines, to the intent to fight with his enemies, so that all manner of people, such as desired honour, drew to the one part and to the other as they owed their service or favour. . . . . This siege endured a long season, the space of eleven weeks all but three days, and all that season the lady Jane of Valois, sister to the French king and mother of the earl of Hainault, toiled greatly to have a respite and a peace between the parties, so that they might depart without battle; and divers times she knelt at the feet of the French king in that behalf, and also made great labour to the lords of the empire, and especially to the duke of Brabant and to the duke of Juliers, who had her daughter in marriage, and also to sir John of Hainault; so much the good lady procured that it was granted that each party should send four sufficient persons to treat on some good way to accord the parties, and a truce for three days; those appointed should meet in a little chapel standing in the fields called Espléchin. At the day appointed these persons met and the good lady with them; of the French party there was Charles king of Bohemia, Charles earl of Alençon, brother to the French king, and the bishop of Liège, the earl of Flanders, and the earl of Armagnac; of the English party there was the duke of Brabant, the bishop of

Lincoln, the duke of Gueldres, the duke of Juliers,
and sir John of Hainault; and when they were
all met, they made each to other great salutations,
and then entered into their treaty; and all that
day they communed on divers ways of accord, and
always the good lady of Valois was among them,
desiring effectually all the parties that they would
do their labour to make a peace; howbeit, the
first day passed without anything doing, and so
they returned and promised to meet again the next
day; the which day they came together again in
the same place and so fell again into their treaty;
and so fell unto certain points agreeable, but it
was then so late that they could not put it in
writing that day; and the third day they met again,
and so finally accorded on a truce to endure for
a year between all parties and all their men; and
also between them that were in Scotland, and all
such as made war in Gascony, Poitou, and in
Saintonge. . . . .
This truce forthwith was cried in both hosts, whereof
the Brabanters were right glad, for they were sore
weary with so long lying at the siege; so that the
next day, as soon as it was daylight, ye should
have seen tents taken down, chariots charged, and
people removed so quick, that a man would have
thought to have seen a new world. Thus the good
town of Tournay was safe, without any great
damage; howbeit, they within endured great pain;
their victuals began to fail; for they had then
scant to serve them, for three or four days at the

most. The king of England departed sore against his mind, if he might have done otherwise, but he was fain to follow the wills of the other lords and to believe their counsels. And the French king could abide no longer where he lay for the evil air and the hot weather, so the Frenchmen had the honour of that journey because they had rescued Tournay and caused their enemies to depart. The king of England and the lords on his party said how they had the honour by reason that they had tarried so long within the realm, and besieged one of the good towns thereof, and had also wasted and burned in the French country, and that the French king had not rescued it in time and hour, as he ought to have done by giving of battle, and had finally agreed to a truce, his enemies being still at the siege and burning his country. Thus these lords departed from the siege of Tournay, and every man drew to his own, and the king of England came to Ghent to the queen, his wife.

1340-1.—How the king returned to London and removed his ministers.

Murimuth, p. 109.

Afterwards when all the English who were with the king at Ghent, believed that the king of England would celebrate Christmas there, the king feigning he was going out for exercise, rode off secretly with only eight attendants, and scarcely telling any of his friends came to Zeeland, and went on board. He sailed for three days and nights and on the night of S. Andrew's, about cockcrow, entered the tower of

London by water; and with him were the earl of
Northampton, the lord Walter of Manny, . . .
and a few others. And immediately at cockcrow he
sent for the chancellor, treasurer, and justices then
present in London; and immediately removed the
bishop of Chichester from the office of chancellor,
and the bishop of Coventry from the office of
treasurer, and he wished to send them into
Flanders and put them in pledge there, or if they
refused this, to keep them against their will in
the tower of London. But the bishop of Chichester
explained to him the danger which he incurred from
the canon which threatens those who imprison
bishops, and so he allowed them to leave the Tower.
But the chief justices, namely the lord John of
Stonor, the lord William of Willoughby, the lord
William of Shereshull, and especially the lord
Nicolas de la Beche who before was warden of the
tower of London, as well as the merchants, the lord
John of Pultenay, William de la Pole and Richard
his brother, and the chief clerks of the chancery,
namely the lords John of S. Paul, Michael of Wath,
Henry of Stretford, Robert of Chikwelle, and of the
treasury the lord Thomas of Thorpe and many
others, he caused to be committed to divers prisons.
But since this had been done wilfully and arbitrarily
by an angry whim, they were presently released.
Also, upon the arrival of the king, John archbishop
of Canterbury* was publicly accused of ingratitude

* John Stratford, since 1333 archbishop of Canterbury, and
his brother Robert, since 1337 bishop of Chichester, had acted
as chancellors alternately for the last ten years.

and other offences by William of Killesby by word of mouth at the Guildhall at London, and afterwards by royal letters; from which charges he declared he was ready to clear himself at the parliament then following, as will appear below. . .

Soon after his arrival the king removed all the sheriffs and other officers and put others in their stead even against their will; and he made a certain knight chancellor of England, namely Robert of Bourchier, and another treasurer, namely first the lord Robert of Sadyton, and afterwards the lord Robert Parvenk, and took the counsel of the young contemning the counsel of the elders. And he ordained that in each county justices should sit, and make enquiry about the collection of the tenth, and of the fifteenth, and of the wool, and all others. And in each county he ordained one great justice, namely an earl or a great baron, to whom he joined others of middle estate; and these justices acted so severely and wilfully that no one escaped unhurt, whether he had done the king's business well or ill: so that without any offence all, even without being indicted or accused, must redeem themselves at excessive fines, if they wished to escape imprisonment, nor would they allow anyone to prove his innocence.

1341.—How the king held his parliament at London and of certain statutes there passed.

Murimuth, p. 112.

(In this parliament the king was obliged to recognise the right of peers to be tried by their peers, as well as to promise that accounts should be audited and ministers sworn to do justice, in parliament. But this statute he revoked the same year.)

In the year of our Lord 1341, in the 15th year of king Edward the third from the Conquest, that king held his parliament at London a fortnight after Easter, wherein the prelates, earls, and great men, to wit the peers and commonalty of the realm, joined in making many good petitions on behalf of the community of the realm, and especially that the Great Charter and the charter of the forest, and the liberties of the church should be wholly maintained ; and that those who offended against them, even if they were officers of the king, should be punished, and that the greater officers of the king should be elected by the peers of the realm in parliament. To these the king with his privy council long refused to consent, and so the parliament lasted to the vigil of Whitsunday. But finally the king granted the greater part of the said petitions, but did not grant the appointment and election of his officers ; he finally however conceded that the officials should swear in parliament that they would do justice in all their offices, and that if they did not do this, they should resign their offices, on the third day after the beginning of parliament and reply to all their accusers, and that the guilty should be punished by the judgment of their peers. Upon all which and other matters a statute was made and sealed with the king's seal. And then license was given to the prelates and others to leave ; but the bishops of Durham and Salisbury, the earls of Salisbury, Warwick, and Northampton were assigned to hear the answer of the archbishop to the charges brought against him and to report to the king in the next parliament. And although the archbishop said he was ready to immediately shew and prove himself innocent, these earls and barons declared they had not then leisure ; and so the business remained in suspense.

1341.—Writ revoking a statute.

Rymer, 1177.

The king, to the sheriff of Lincoln, greeting. Whereas in our parliament assembled at Westminster, on the fifteenth day of Easter last past, certain articles expressly contrary to the laws and customs of our realm of England, and to our royal right and prerogatives, are pretended to have been conceded by us by manner of statute :

We, considering how we are bound by oath to observe and defend such laws, customs, rights, and prerogatives, and therefore wishing to recall to the due state those things which have been improvidently done, have taken counsel and have treated upon this with the earls, barons, and otherwise men of our realm :

And because we never consented to the issue of the pretended statute, but having first protested that we would recall the said statute if it actually proceeded, to avoid the perils which it was then feared would arise from refusal since that parliament would otherwise have dissolved in discord without having done anything, and so our arduous business would have been truly ruined, we dissembled as was

]
]
i
1
s

\
c
a
o
p
u

o
p
d
d
w

th
w
ce
w
ot
dc
ha

fitting, and permitted the pretended statute to be then sealed; it seemed good to the said earls, barons, and wise men that, since the aforesaid pretended statute did not proceed from our free will, it should be null, and ought not to have the name or force of a statute :

And, therefore, the said statute, with their counsel and consent, we decree to be null and have judged that so far as it has gone it ought to be annulled:

Desiring, however, that the articles contained in the said pretended statute which have been previously approved by other statutes of us or our progenitors, kings of England, shall be observed, according to the form of the said statutes, in all things, as is fitting. And this only we do for the preservation and restoration of the rights of our crown as we are bound, not that we would in any way oppress or grieve our subjects, whom we wish to rule in mildness.

And, therefore, we order you that you cause all this to be publicly proclaimed in such places within your district as you see to be suitable.

Witness the king at Westminster, the first day of October.   By the king and council.

Similar writs were directed to all the sheriffs throughout England.

1342.—How the countess of Montfort defended Hennebon.

Froissart, ch. 80 (I. §§ 165-166). *Jehan le Bel*, ch. 54.

(The duchy of Brittany was disputed between John of Montfort, who was supported by Edward of England, and Charles of Blois, supported by Philip of France.   Montfort had been taken prisoner, but his wife Joan gallantly carried on the struggle. For the rival claims, see *Appendix.*)

.   .   .   . The countess herself wore harness on her body, and rode on a great charger from street to street, desiring her people to make good defence ; and she caused damsels and other women to cut short their kirtles and to carry stones and pots full of chalk to the walls, to be cast down to their enemies. This lady did there a hardy enterprise.   She mounted up to the height of a tower to see how the Frenchmen were ordered without ; she saw how that the lords and all the other people of the host were all gone out of their camp to the assault.   She issued out with her company and dashed into the French lodgings, and cut down tents and set fire to their lodgings.   She found no defence there but certain varlets and boys who ran away.   When the lords of France looked behind them and saw their lodgings afire and heard the cry and noise there, they returned to the camp, crying, "Treason ! treason !" so that all the assault was left.   When the countess saw that, she drew together her company, and when she saw she could not enter again into the town without great damage, she took another way and went to the castle of Brest, the which was not far thence. When sir Louis of Spain, who was marshal of the host, was come to the camp and saw the countess and her company going away he followed after her with a great number ; he chased her so near that he slew and hurt divers of them that were behind, evil horsed. But the countess and the most part of her company rode so well that they came to Brest, and there they were received with great joy. . . . . The next day the lords of France, who had lost their tents and their provisions, then took counsel to lodge in bowers of trees nearer to the town, and they had great marvel when they knew that the countess herself had done that enterprise. They of the town wist not where the countess was gone, whereof they were in great trouble, for it was five days ere they heard any tidings. The countess did so much at Brest that she got together five hundred spears; and then about midnight she departed from Brest and by the sun rising she came along by the one side of the host and came to one of the gates of Hennebon, the which was opened for her; and therein she entered and all her company with great noise of trumpets, whereof the French host had great marvel, and armed themselves and ran to the town to assault it, and they within were ready to defend. There began a fierce assault and endured till noon, but the Frenchmen lost more than they within. . . . .

(Some time after, the town was so hard pressed that those within thought of yielding. But just as they are about to give up the town),

Then the countess looked down along the sea out at a window in the castle and began to smile for great joy that she had to see the succours coming, the which she had so long desired. Then she cried

out aloud and said twice, " I see the succours of
England coming!" Then they of the town ran
to the walls and saw a great number of ships, great
and small, freshly decked, coming towards Hennebon. They knew well it was the succours of
England, who had been on the sea sixty days by
reason of contrary winds.

1344.—Of the order of St. George that king Edward established in the castle of Windsor.

Froissart, ch. 100.

In this season the king of England took pleasure
to new re-edify the castle of Windsor. . . . .
Then king Edward determined to make an order and
a brotherhood of a certain number of knights, and to
be called knights of the blue garter ; and a feast to
be kept yearly at Windsor on St. George's day. And
to begin this order the king assembled together
earls, lords, and knights of his realm and shewed
them his intention ; and they all joyously agreed to
his pleasure, because they saw it was a thing much
honourable and whereby great amity and love should
grow and increase. Then were there chosen out a
certain number of the valiantest men of the realm,
and they swore to maintain the ordinances such as
were devised ; and the king made a chapel in the
castle of Windsor, of St. George, and stablished
certain canons there to serve God, and endowed
them with fair rent. Then the king sent to publish
this feast by his heralds, into France, Scotland,
Burgundy, Hainault, Flanders, Brabant, and into the

empire of Almayne, giving to every knight and squire that would come to the said feast, 15 days of safe conduct before the feast and after the feast, to begin at Windsor on St. George's day next after, in the year of our Lord 1344, and the queen to be there, accompanied with 300 ladies and damsels, all of noble lineage and apparelled accordingly.

1345.—Of the death of Jacques d'Artevelde of Ghent.

Froissart, ch. 115 (I. § 237).

(The truces were ill observed and a renewal of the war was inevitable. Edward therefore crossed to Flanders and attempted to secure a firm basis of operations in Flanders by getting his son accepted as its earl).

In this season reigned in Flanders, in great prosperity and puissance, Jacques d'Artevelde of Ghent, who was as great with the king of England as he could desire : and he had promised the king to make him lord and heritor of Flanders, and to endue his son, the prince of Wales, therewith, and to make the county of Flanders a dukedom. For which cause about the feast of St. John Baptist, 1345, the king of England was come to Sluys, and had brought thither the young prince. The king with all his navy lay in the haven of Sluys, and thither came to visit him his friends of Flanders ; then were great councils between the king and Jacques d'Artevelde on the one side, and the councils of the good men of Flanders on the other ; so that they of the country were not agreed with the king nor with Jacques d'Artevelde, who preached to them that they should

disinherit the earl Louis, their own natural lord and
also his young son Louis. And so the last day of
their council on the king's great ship the Katherine,
they gave a final answer by common accord and said,
"Sir, ye have desired us to a thing that is great and
weighty, which hereafter may sore touch the county
of Flanders and our heirs. Truly we know not at
this day no person in the world that we love the
preferment of, so much as we do yours. But, sir,
this thing we cannot do alone, without that all the
commonalty of Flanders accord to the same ; sir, we
will go home, and every man speak with his company
in every town, and as the most part may agree we
shall be content; and within a month we shall be
here with you again, and then give you a full
answer." Jacques d'Artevelde tarried a little season,
with the king, and still he promised the king to
bring them to his intent ; but he was deceived, for
as soon as he came to Ghent he went no more out
again ; for such of Ghent as had been at Sluys at the
council there, when they were returned to Ghent,
ere Jacques d'Artevelde was come into the town,
great and small they assembled in the market place,
and then it was openly shewed what request the king
of England had made to them, by the setting on of
Jacques d'Artevelde ; then every man began to
murmur against Jacques, for that request pleased
them nothing.

When Jacques returned, he came to Ghent about
noon. They of the town knew of his coming, and
many were assembled in the street where he should

pass, and when they saw him they began to murmur and said, "Behold yonder great master, that will order all Flanders after his pleasure, which is not to be suffered." Also then were words sown through all the town, how he had nine years assembled all the revenues of Flanders without any account given, and thereby had kept his state, and also sent great riches out of the country into England secretly. These words set them of Ghent on fire, and as he rode through the street he perceived there was some new matter against him, for such as were wont to make reverence to him he saw them turn their backs towards him and enter into their houses. Then he began to doubt; and as soon as he had alighted at his lodging, he closed fast his gates, doors, and windows. This was scant done before the street was full of men, and specially of them of the small crafts. They assailed his house both behind and before, and the house was broken into. He and his within defended themselves a long space, and slew and hurt many without; but finally he could not endure, for three parts of the men of the town were at the assault. When Jacques saw that he was so sore oppressed, he came to a window, with great humility, bare-headed, and said with fair language, "Good people, what aileth you? why be ye so sore troubled against me? in what manner have I displeased you? shew me and I will make you amends." Then such as heard him answered all with one voice, "We will have account made of the great treasure of Flanders that ye have sent out of the way, without any title of reason." Then Jacques answered meekly, " Certainly, sirs, of the treasure of Flanders I never took anything : withdraw yourselves patiently into your houses and come again to-morrow in the morning, and I shall give you so good account that of reason ye shall be content." Then all they answered and said, " Nay, we will have account given immediately, ye shall not escape us so ; we know for truth that ye have sent great riches into England, without our knowledge ; wherefore ye shall die." When he heard that word, he joined his hands together, and sore weeping said, " Sirs, such as I am ye have made me, and ye have sworn to me, ere this, to defend me against all persons, and now ye would slay me without reason ; ye may do it, an ye will, for I am but one man among you all. For God's sake take better advice, and remember the time past. Ye know right well merchandise was nigh lost in all this country, and by my means it is recovered. I have governed you in great peace and rest, for ye have had all things that ye could wish, corn, riches, and all other merchandise." Then they all cried with one voice, " Come down to us, and preach not so high, and give us account of the great treasure of Flanders." When Jacques saw that he could not appease them, he drew in his head, and closed his window, and so thought to steal out on the back side into a church that joined to his house, but his house was so broken that four hundred persons were entered into his house, and finally then he was taken and slain without mercy, and one Thomas Denys gave him his death stroke.

Thus Jacques d' Artevelde ended his days, who had been a great master in Flanders: poor men first mounteth up, and unhappy men slayeth them at the end.

(Edward thereupon returned to England).

1345. — Of the failure of the great and powerful company of the Bardi.

Giovanni Villani, Istorie Fiorentine, l. xii., c. liv.

In the year 1345 in the month of January failed the company of the Bardi, who had been the greatest merchants in Italy. And the reason was that they, like the Peruzzi, had lent their money and that invested with them to king Edward of England and to the king of Sicily; and that the Bardi found they had owing to them from the king of England, what with capital and interest and gifts promised by him, 900,000 florins of gold,* and on account of his war with the king of France he was unable to pay; and from the king of Sicily 100,000 florins of gold. And to the Peruzzi were owing from the king of England 600,000 florins of gold, and from the king of Sicily 100,000 florins of gold, and a debt of 350,000 florins of gold, so they must stop payment to citizens and foreigners, to whom the Bardi alone owed more than 550,000 florins of gold. Whereby many other smaller companies and individuals whose money was in the hands of the Bardi or Peruzzi or others who had failed, were ruined and so became bankrupt. By this failure of the Bardi, Peruzzi, Acciajuoli, and

* The florin was one-eighth of an ounce of gold.

Bonaccorsi . . of the company of Uzzano Peran-doli, and many other small companies and individual craftsmen, owing to the burdens on the state and the disordered loans to lords, of which I have made mention (though not of all, which were too long to tell), came greater ruin and discomfiture to our city of Florence than any our state had received, if the reader well consider the damage caused by such a loss of treasure and money lost by our citizens, and lent from avarice to lords. O cursed and greedy usury, full of the vice of avarice reigning in our blind and mad citizens of Florence, who from covetousness to gain from great lords put their wealth and that of others in their power and lordship to lose, and ruin our republic; for there remained no substance of money in our citizens, except in a few craftsmen and lenders who with their usury consumed and gained for themselves the scattered poverty of our citizens and subjects. But not without cause come to states and citizens the secret judgments of God, to punish the sins which have been committed, as Christ with his own mouth said in the gospel "Ye shall die in your sin." The Bardi agreed to give up to their creditors their possessions, which they estimated would come to 9 shillings and 3 pence in the pound, but at a fair price did not come to six shillings in the pound

1346.—How the king of England came over the sea again.

Froissart, ch. 121. (I. §§ 254-5.)

(In spite of a victory of the earl of Derby at Auberoche, in

1345, the French seemed about to conquer Guienne and were besieging Aiguillon.)

The king of England, who had heard how his men were sore constrained in the castle of Aiguillon, thought to go over the sea into Gascony with a great army. In the same season, the lord Godfrey of Harcourt, who was banished out of France, came into England. He was well received with the king, and retained to be about him, and had fair lands assigned him in England to maintain his degree. Then the king caused a great navy of ships to be ready in the haven of [South] Hampton, and caused all manner of men of war to draw thither. About the feast of St. John Baptist, the year of our Lord God, 1346, the king departed from the queen, and left her in the guiding of the earl of Kent his cousin, and he stablished the lord Percy and the lord Neville to be wardens of his realm, with the archbishop of York, the bishop of Lincoln and the bishop of Durham; for he never left his realm but he left ever enough at home to keep and defend his realm, if need were. Then the king rode to Hampton and there tarried for wind. Then he entered into his ship, and the prince of Wales with him, the lord Godfrey of Harcourt, and all other lords, barons, and knights, with all their companies; they were in number four thousand men of arms, and ten thousand archers, beside Irishmen and Welshmen that followed the host afoot. Thus they sailed forth that day, in the name of God. They were well on their way toward Gascony, but on the third day there arose a contrary wind and drave them

on Cornwall, and there they lay at anchor six days.
In that space the king had other counsel from sir
Godfrey Harcourt.   He counselled the king not to
go to Gascony, but rather to set a-land in Normandy,
and said, "Sir, the country of Normandy is one of
the plenteous countries of the world.   On jeopardy
of my head, if ye will land there, there is none that
will resist you ; the people of Normandy have not
been used to the war, and all the knights and squires
of the country are now at the siege before Aiguillon.
And sir, there ye shall find great towns that be not
walled, whereby your men shall have such winning
that they shall be the better thereby twenty years
after."   The king who was then but in the flower of
his youth, desiring nothing so much as to have deed
of arms, inclined greatly to the saying of the lord of
Harcourt whom he called cousin; then he commanded
the mariners to set their course to Normandy and
arrived in the isle of Cotentin, at a port called la
Hogue.

(He took Caen, and then marched east to join the Flemings;
but Philip, who had gathered a great army and in vain tried to
prevent his crossing the Seine, came up with him at Crecy, near
Abbeville).

1346, Aug.—Of the order of the Englishmen at Crecy.

Froissart, ch. 128 (I. § 274).

On the Friday the king of England lay in the
fields, for the country was plentiful in wines and
other victual, and if need had been they had provision

following in carts and other carriages. That night the king made a supper to all his chief lords of his host, and made them good cheer. And when they were all departed to take their rest, then the king entered into his oratory, and kneeled down before the altar, praying God devoutly that if he fought the next day he might achieve the enterprise to his honour. Then about midnight he laid him down to rest. And in the morning he rose betimes and heard mass, and the prince his son with him, and the most part of his company were confessed and houseled. And, after the mass said, he commanded every man to be armed, and to draw to the field to the same place before appointed. Then the king caused a fenced place to be made by the wood side, behind his host, and there were set all carts and carriages, and within this park were all their horses, for every man was afoot. And into this park there was but one entry. Then he ordained three lines of battle. In the first was the young prince of Wales, and with him was the earl of Warwick and divers other knights and squires. They were eight hundred men of arms and two thousand archers, and a thousand others with the Welshmen; every lord drew to the field appointed under his own banner and pennon. In the second line of battle was the earl of Northampton, the earl of Arundel, and divers others, about eight hundred men of arms and twelve hundred archers. The third line had the king; he had seven hundred men of arms and two thousand archers. Then the king leapt on a palfrey with a white rod in

his hand, one of his marshals on the one hand and
the other on the other hand ; he rode from rank to
rank, desiring every man to take heed that day to his
right and honour.   He spake it so sweetly and with
so good countenance and merry cheer that all such
as were discomfited took courage in the seeing and
hearing of him.   And when he had thus visited each
line of battle, it was then nine of the day.   Then he
caused every man to eat and drink a little, and so
they did at their leisure.   And afterwards they ordered
again their battles ; then every man lay down on the
earth, and by him his helmet and bow, to be the
fresher when their enemies should come.

**1346.—The order of the Frenchmen at Crecy and
how they beheld the demeanour of the Englishmen.**

Froissart, ch. 129 (I. §§ 275-7).   *Jehan le Bel*, ch. 72.

This Saturday the French king rose betimes and
heard mass in Abbeville, in his lodging in the abbey
of Saint Peter ; and he departed after the sunrising.
When he was out of the town two leagues,
approaching toward his enemies, some of his lords
said to him, " Sir, it were good that you arranged
your lines of battle, and let all your foot men pass
somewhat on before, that they be not troubled with
the horsemen."   Then the king sent four knights,
. . . . to ride to view the English host.   And
so they rode so near that they might well see part
of their dealing.   The Englishmen saw them well,
and knew well how they were come thither to view
them ; they let them alone, and made no countenance

toward them, and let them return as they came. And when the French king saw these four knights return again, he tarried till they came to him, and said, "Sirs, what tidings?" These four knights each of them looked on the other, for there was none would speak before his companion; finally, the king said to Moine, who belonged to the king of Bohemia, and had done in his days so much that he was reputed for one of the valiantest knights of the world, "Sir, speak you." Then he said, "Sir, I shall speak since it pleaseth you, under the correction of my fellows. Sir, we have ridden and seen the behaving of your enemies; know you that they are rested in three lines of battle, abiding for you. Sir, I will counsel you, as for my part, saving your displeasure, that you and all your company rest here and lodge for this night; for ere they that be behind of your company be come hither, and ere your lines be set in good order it will be very late, and your people be weary and out of array, and you shall find your enemies fresh and ready to receive you. Early in the morning you may order your lines at more leisure, and consider your enemies with more deliberation, and regard well what way ye will assail them; for, sir, surely they will abide you." Then the king commanded that it should be done. Then his two marshals one rode before and another behind, saying to every banner, "Tarry and abide here in the name of God and Saint Denis." They that were foremost tarried, but they that were behind would not tarry but rode forth, and said how they would in no wise abide until they were as far forward as the foremost. And when they before saw them come on behind, then they rode forward again, so that neither the king nor his marshals could rule them; so they rode without order or good array till they came in sight of their enemies. . . . . When they saw that they were near to their enemies, they took their swords and cried, "Down with them! let us slay them all!" There was no man, though he were present at the journey, that could imagine or show the truth of the evil order that was among the French party, and yet they were a marvellous great number. What I write in this book, I learned it specially of the Englishmen who well beheld their dealing, and also certain knights of sir John of Hainault, who was always about king Philip, shewed me as they knew.

1346.—Of the battle of Crecy between the king of England and the French king.

Freissart, ch. 130 (I. §§ 277-280, 283).

The Englishmen, who were in three lines of battle lying on the ground to rest them, as soon as they saw the Frenchmen approach, rose upon their feet, fair and easily without any haste, and arranged their lines. The first was the prince's division; the archers there stood in manner of a harrow, and the men of arms in the bottom of the division. The earl of Northampton and the earl of Arundel with the second line were on a wing in good order, ready to comfort the prince's line if need were. The lords

and knights of France came not to the assembly
together in good order, for some came before and
some came after, in such haste and evil order that
one of them did trouble another. When the French
king saw the Englishmen, his blood changed, and he
said to his marshals, "Make the Genoese go on
before and begin the battle, in the name of God and
Saint Denis." There were of the Genoese crossbow-
men about fifteen thousand; but they were so weary
of going afoot that day six leagues armed with their
crossbows, that they said to their constables, "We
be not well ordered to fight this day, for we be not
in the case to do any great deed of arms; we have
more need of rest." These words came to the earl
of Alençon, who said, "A man is well at ease
to be charged with such a sort of rascals, who faint
and fail now at most need." Also the same season
there fell a great rain, with thunder and lightning
very great and horrible. And before the rain there
came flying over both armies a great number of
crows for fear of the tempest coming. Then anon
the air began to wax clear, and the sun to shine fair
and bright; the which was right in the Frenchmen's
eyes, and on the Englishmen's backs. When the
Genoese were assembled together and began to
approach, they made a great leap and cry to abash
the Englishmen, but they stood still and stirred not
for all that. Then the Genoese again, the second
time, made another leap and a fell cry, and stepped
forward a little, and the Englishmen removed not
one foot. Thirdly again they leapt and cried and

went forth till they came within shot. Then they shot fiercely with their crossbows. Then the English archers stept forth one pace and let fly their arrows altogether, and so thick that it seemed snow. When the Genoese felt the arrows piercing through heads, arms, and breasts, many of them cast down their crossbows, and did cut their strings, and returned discomfited. When the French king saw them flee away, he said, " Slay these rascals, for they will hinder and trouble us without reason." Then you should have seen the men of arms dash in among them, and they killed a great number of them. And ever still the Englishmen shot as they saw thickest press ; the sharp arrows ran into the men of arms and into their horses ; and many fell, horse and men, among the Genoese ; and when they were down they could not rise again ; the press was so thick that one overthrew another. And also among the Englishmen there were certain rascals that went afoot, with great knives, and they went in among the men of arms, and slew and murdered many as they lay on the ground, both earls, barons, knights, and squires ; whereof the king of England was after displeased, for he had rather they had been taken prisoners. The valiant king of Bohemia, called John of Luxemburg, son to the noble emperor Henry of Luxemburg, for all that he was nigh blind, when he understood the order of the battle, he said to them about him, " Where is the lord Charles my son ?" His men said, " Sir, we cannot tell ; we think he is fighting." Then he said, " Sirs, ye are my men,

WINDMILL HILL AT CRECY.

my companions and friends in this enterprise; I
require you bring me so forward that I may strike
one stroke with my sword." They said they would
do his commandment; and to the intent that they
should not lose him in the press, they tied all their
reins of their bridles each to other, and set the king
before to accomplish his desire; and so they went
on their enemies. The lord Charles, his son, who
wrote himself king of Germany, came in good order
to the battle; but when he saw the matter went awry
on their part, he departed I cannot tell you which
way. The king his father was so far forward that he
struck a stroke with his sword, yea and more than
four, and fought valiantly. And so did his company,
and they adventured themselves so forward that they
were all slain, and the next day they were found in
the place about the king, and all their horses tied
each to other. . . . .
The day of the battle certain Frenchmen and
Germans perforce opened the archers of the prince's
battalion, and came and fought with the men at
arms, hand to hand. Then the second division of
the Englishmen came to succour the prince's
division, the which was time, for they had then
much ado. And they with the prince sent a
messenger to the king, who was on a little windmill
hill. Then the knight said to the king, "Sir, the
earl of Warwick, sir Reynold Cobham, and other
such as be about the prince, your son, are fiercely
fought withal and are sore handled; wherefore they
desire you that you and your division will come

and aid them, for if the Frenchmen increase, as they fear they will, your son and they shall have much ado." Then the king said, "Is my son dead, or hurt, or on the earth felled?" "No, sir," quoth the knight, "but he is hardly matched, wherefore he hath need of your aid." "Well," said the king, "return to him and to them that sent you hither, and say to them that they send no more to me for any adventure that falleth, so long as my son is alive; and also say to them that they suffer him this day to win his spurs, for, if God be pleased, I will this day to be his and the honour thereof, and to them that be about him." Then the knight returned again to them and shewed the king's words, the which greatly encouraged them; and they repined in that they had sent to the king as they did. . . . .

In the evening the French king had left about him no more than threescore persons, whereof sir John of Hainault was one, who had remounted once the king, for his horse was slain with an arrow. Then sir John of Hainault said to the king, "Sir, depart hence, for it is time; lose not yourself wilfully. If you have lost at this time, ye shall recover it again another season." And so he took the king's horse by the bridle and led him away in a manner perforce. Then the king rode till he came to the castle of Broyes. The gate was closed, because it was by that time dark. Then the king called the captain, who came to the walls and said, "Who is it that calleth there, this time of night?" Then the king said,

"Open your gate quickly, for this is the fortune of France." The captain knew then it was the king, and opened the gate and let down the bridge. The king would not tarry there, but drank and departed thence about midnight; and so rode by such guides as knew the country well till he came in the morning to Amiens, and there he rested. This Saturday the Englishmen never departed from their ranks for chasing of any man, but kept still their field and ever defended themselves against all such as came to assail them. This battle ended about evensong time.

1346, Oct.—Battle of Neville's Cross.

Chron. of Lanercost, 347-357.

(After the English had failed to take Dunbar, the party of Bruce in Scotland had re-won the greater part of the kingdom, and in 1341 the young David Bruce returned from France. Edward again led an army into Scotland, but could effect nothing; and in March, 1345, a truce was agreed to. In the summer of 1346 at the instigation of Philip of France, David invaded the Northern counties of England, but was met near Durham by the archbishop of York and lords Neville and Percy, the wardens of the Border).

Now on the fourteenth day of October the bishop set out with his host from Richmond, and marched with all speed by the straight way unto Castle Barnard; on the morrow, in the neighbourhood of this same castle, he and the other chiefs held a reckoning of their men of arms, horsemen and footmen, knights and esquires; for there was there a little hill having a level summit. Moreover in the

same place the commanders did ordain the arraying
of the host, and all else that was fitting.   Accordingly
they parted themselves into three strong divisions,
whereof the lord Henry Percy led the first, the lord
Thomas of Rokeby the second, but the third the
bishop of York himself commanded, like a wise
father, a pure and holy shepherd of his sheep.   And
so all the host, not in hatred as was Cain when he
slew his brother, nor yet in vain glory as was
Absalom when the tree caught him up, marched
with due care towards the town of Auckland, putting
their trust not in sword or helm, in spear or hauberk,
or other golden armour, but altogether upon the
name of Christ, and knowing beside that they were
not going to attack others, but to resist them that
had come against them: and that same night they
pitched their tents in a certain fair wood and there
the army of England awaited the day.   Now at the
dawning of the morrow, which was the vigil of St.
Luke the evangelist, William of Douglas and fifty
others with him went forth from the Scottish host to
harry the country and get them plunder ; whereby it
came to pass that the spoil, which the Scotch took
in the morning, the English parted among themselves
in the evening.   For on that morning, while the
Scots were wasting the village of Merrington, there
fell on them suddenly tempestuous weather and
dense clouds.   Besides this, there came to their
ears the tramp of steeds and the clash of armour,
whence there fell on them so sudden a plague of fear
that William and all his men knew not whither they

should turn. So, as God willed, smitten with terror at this sudden chance, they stumbled upon the division of the lord archbishop of York and the lord Thomas of Rokeby. Thereby many of them were slain, but William and two hundred with him, who were on tried horses, escaped for that time, though not unhurt. Then Robert of Ogle, a man of great strength, and by no means untrained in the arts of war, followed after them over hill and plain, and many he slew with his own hand, nor would he stay until his steed, out-worn by exceeding toil, stopped at a great stream at the bottom of a wooded vale and could go no further. Then came William much heated to the Scottish host, and cried aloud with much fervor of heart: "David, quick up! all the Englishmen are upon us." But David made answer that it could not be; "There are not left," he said, "in England but wretched monks, impious priests, swineherds, tailors, and cobblers; these dare not face me, I am safe enough"; nathless they faced him, and, as was afterwards made plain, handled him right well. "Of a truth," answered William, "most honoured king, saving your peace, you will not find it so; they are many. and mighty men, and come against us with all speed and are eager after battle." Now, immediately before these words, had come two Black Monks of them of Durham to treat with David for a truce. "See then," said David, "with what guile do these false monks speak with us; therefore did they hold us in conclave,

8

that suddenly the English host should come upon us, thus caught in their toils." Wherefore he bade seize them at once, and behead them, but at that time the Scots were so busied that the monks fled unseen, and with much joy and no harm made their way safely back to their own place. On this wise did David, more foolish than a fool, endeavour to catch the fish, ere he had a net, whereby he lost many and caught but few; nor did he keep to the purpose which he had purposed, and like another Haman or Achitophel, what he had designed for us fell on his own head. Then, viewing his people David gathered the Scots together, (folk that were to be scattered, as the event willed,) and, like a second Jabin against Joshua, arrayed three great and strong divisions to front the Englishmen. In the first rank he set the earl Patrick, but he, like a man of no skill, begged not to have the leadership. And that post the earl of Moray forthwith obtained, and thus in the first rank of the army he held the chief place, and there afterwards he fell in the fray. With him were many valiant men of Scotland, as the earl of Strathern, the earl of Fife, John of Douglas the brother of lord William of Douglas, the lord Alexander of Ramsay, and many other valiant earls and barons, knights and squires, furiously raging, of unbridled spirit, all of one mind against the English, nor would they stay from their headlong course, but firmly trusting in their own power, and rising with overweening pride thought, like Satan, to reach the stars. The second division David the king led himself, not him of whom

the choirs sang that he had turned to flight his ten
thousands in the war. With him he brought the earl
of Buchan, Malcolm Fleming, lord Alexander of
Strathern, the earl of Monteith, and many another,
whom we know not, and, did we know, it were tedious
to relate. . . . .
About the third hour hard by Durham the English
host came upon the Scotchmen, and then in the first
line the earl of Angus, a man of noble stock, of
great valour and wonderful virtue, was ever ready to
do battle for his country, whose fair feats, indeed,
not one or many tongues could chronicle. The
lord Henry Percy, a good warrior like a second
Judas Maccabeus, a man of low stature but great
wisdom, boldly set his own body in the foremost
ranks and made all bold to spring into the fray.
The lord Ralph of Neville, a truth-speaker and a
valiant man, bold, wise, and fear-worthy, so fought
in that fray that thereafter the dints of his blows
were to be seen on the foe. . . . .

In the second division the lord archbishop of
York was their leader, who called his sons and gave
them his blessing. . . . .

There was also a bishop of the order of the
Minorites, who for a blessing bade the Englishmen
fight like men on pain of much penance, and ordered
that none should spare a Scot. And when he himself met the foe, he spared not for inflicting of
penance or for rebuke, but with a certain staff
gave them indulgences, penances, and proper abso-
lution ; such power had he then that with his staff,

without any confession heard, he absolved the Scots of all future trouble in this world. . . . . In the third division was the lord John of Mowbray. . . . . The lord Thomas of Rokeby, like a good leader, pledged the Scots in such liquor as, when they had once tasted, they desired no more trial of it, and stood forth in all men's eyes as an example of one who warred bravely for his country. . . . Thus amid the blare of trumpets, the clashing of shields, the hurtling of arrows, you might have heard spears flying, and the wailing of the wounded. Arms were shattered, heads broken, many, alas, slain on the field. Before the hour of vespers the battle came to an end. The Scots fled and our men slew them; all praise to the Highest, Who on that day gave the victory to the English. And thus, by the prayers of the Blessed Virgin Mary and of Saint Cuthbert, the confessor of Christ, David and the flower of Scotland fell by the just judgment of God into the pit which they themselves had digged. David, who called himself king of Scotland, was taken, and not long after, with many nobler captives, was brought to London and there thrown into prison.

1346.—Song of Neville's Cross.

By Laurence Minot [Political Poems (Rolls Series) 1. 83].

Sir David had of his men great loss
With sir Edward at Neville's Cross.

Sir David the Bruce,
   Would strive, did he say,
To ride through all England,
   For naught would he stay.

At Westminster Hall
   Should his steeds stand
Whilst our king Edward
   Was out of the land.

But now hath sir David
   Missed of his marks,
And Philip of Valois
   With all their great clerks.

Sir Philip the Valois,
   Sooth for to say,
Sent unto sir David
   And fair 'gan him pray,

To ride through all England
   Their foemen to slay,
And said " none is at home
   To hinder the way."

None hinders his way
   To wend where he will,
But with shepherds' staves
   Found he his fill.

From Philip the Valois
   Was sir David sent,
All England to win,
   From Tweed unto Trent.

He brought many bagmen,
  Ready bent was their bow,
They robbed and they ravaged
  And nought they let go.

.   .   .   .

But shamed were the knaves
  And sad must they feel,
For at Neville's Cross
  Needs must they kneel.

Of the archbishop of York
  Now will I begin,
For he may with his right hand
  Absolve us of sin.

Both Durham and Carlisle
  They would never blin*
The worship of England
  With weapons to win.

Mickle worship they won,
  And well have they waken,
For sir David the Bruce
  Was in that time taken.

When sir David the Bruce
  Sat on his steed,
He said of all England
  Had he no dread.

But brave John of Copland,
  A man gay in weed,
Talked to sir David
  And learned him his creed.

* Cease.

There was sir David,
  So doughty in deed,
The fair town of London
  Had he as his meed.

Soon was sir David
  Brought into the Tower,
And William the Douglas,
  With men of honour.

. . . .

Sir David the Bruce
  Maketh his moan,
The fair crown of Scotland
  All hath he foregone.

He looked unto France
  And help had he none
Of sir Philip the Valois
  Nor yet of sir John.

. . . .

The Scots with their falsehood
  Thus went they about
All for to win England
  Whilst Edward was out.

1346.—How Douglas breakfasted at Tynemouth.

Chronicle of St. Albans, ii. 378.

Now heavier troubles came on Thomas, the prior
of Tynemouth; for the king of Scotland, called
David the Bruce, taking courage at the absence of
king Edward, who at that time was fighting against
Philip king of France at Crecy, and prompted by

letters from the said Philip, collected an army, entered
the country, killed several, captured many, burnt
farms, destroyed provisions, demanded ransom for
goods, and did innumerable evils.   But Thomas,
amid these dangers, remained unbent, and put his
priory in readiness with men, arms, provisions, and
instruments of war, in such a way that the enemy
would not be able to do hurt without great difficulty
and peril to themselves.

At that time William Douglas, the leader of the
army, on which was placed all the hope of the Scots,
being a haughty, arrogant, and sarcastic man, sent a
message to Thomas after his fashion, telling him to
get breakfast ready, for in two days he was going to
breakfast with him, so saying of a truth but to
frighten him.   And his saying was fulfilled—for it
was a prophecy like that saying of Caiaphas.   For
two days after, he was taken prisoner, and sent to
Tynemouth for safe custody.   The prior went to
meet him, and jestingly bade him welcome to the
breakfast he had prepared.   Whereat William, " I'm
very angry at coming in this way."   " Nay," said the
prior," you could never be more welcome."

1347, Aug.—How the town of Calais was given up to the king of England.

Froissart, ch. 146 (I. § 311).   *Jehan le Bel*, chs. 90-91.

(Immediately after Crecy, Edward had laid siege to Calais.
Philip came with an army in the spring of the next year, but was
unable to deliver the town, and withdrew.)

After that the French king was thus departed from

Sangate, they within Càlais saw well how their
succour failed them, for the which they were in
great sorrow. Then they desired so much their
captain, sir John of Vienne, that he went to the
walls of the town, and made a sign to speak with
some person of the host. When the king heard
thereof he sent thither sir Walter of Manny and
sir Basset. Then sir John of Vienne said to them,
"Sirs, ye be right valiant knights in deeds of arms,
and ye know well how the king, my master, hath
sent me and others to this town and commanded
us to keep it on his behalf, in such wise that we
take no blame nor do him no damage; and we
have done all that lieth in our power. Now our
succours have failed us, and we are sore straitened
that we have not wherewithal to live, but we must
all die or else go mad with famine, without the
noble and gentle king of yours will take mercy on
us. Wherefore, we beseech you to desire him to
have pity on us, and to let us go and depart as we
are, and let him take the town and castle and all
the goods that are therein, of which there is great
abundance."

Then sir Walter of Manny said, "Sir, we know
somewhat of the intention of the king, our master,
for he hath shewed it unto us. Surely know for
truth it is not his mind that ye nor they within
the town should depart so, for it is his will that
ye should put yourselves into his pure will to ransom
all such as pleaseth him, and to put to death such
as he list; for they of Calais have done him such

contraries and despites, and have caused him to
spend so much of his goods, and has lost so many
of his men, that he is sore grieved against them."

Then the captain said, "Sir, this is too hard a
matter to us.   We are here within but a small
number of knights and squires, who have truly served
the king, our master, as well as you serve yours in
like case.   And we have endured much pain and
unease ; but we will yet endure as much pain as
ever knight did, rather than to consent that the
worst lad in the town should have any more evil
than the greatest of us all.   Therefore, sir, we pray
you of your humility yet that you will go and speak
to the king of England, and desire him to have
pity on us ; for we trust to find in him so much
gentleness, that by the grace of God his purpose
shall change."   Sir Walter of Manny and sir Basset
returned to the king and declared to him all that
had been said.   The king said he would none otherwise, but that they should yield them up simply to
his pleasure.   Then sir Walter said, " Sir, saving
your displeasure in this, you may be in the wrong,
for you shall give by this an evil example.   If you send
any of us your servants into any fortress, we will not
be very glad to go, if you put any of them in the
town to death after they have yielded, for in likewise
they will deal with us if the case chanced alike."
The which words divers other lords that were present
sustained and maintained.   Then the king said,
" Sirs, I will not be alone against you all ; therefore,
sir Walter of Manny, you shall go and say to the

captain that all the grace that he shall find now
in me is, that they let six of the chief burgesses
of the town come out bare-headed, bare-footed, and
bare-legged and in their shirts, with halters about
their necks, with the keys of the town and castle
in their hands; and let these six yield themselves
purely to my will, and the residue I will take to
mercy." Then sir Walter returned and found sir
John of Vienne still on the wall, abiding for an
answer. Then sir Walter shewed him all the grace
that he could get of the king. "Well," quoth sir
John, "Sir, I beseech you tarry here a certain space
till I go into the town and shew this to the commons
of the town, who sent me hither." Then sir John
went into the Market Place and sounded the common
bell. Then forthwith men and women assembled
there; then the captain made report of all that
he had done, and said, "Sirs, it will be none otherwise, therefore now take advice and make a short
answer." Then all the people began to weep and
to make such sorrow, that there was not so hard
a heart if they had seen them, but that would have
had great pity of them; the captain himself wept
piteously. At last the most rich burgess of all
the town, called Eustace of Saint Peter's, rose up
and said openly, "Sirs, great and small, great
mischief it should be to suffer to die such people
as are in this town, either by famine or otherwise,
when there is a way to save them. I think he
or they should have great merit of our Lord God
that might keep them from such mischief. As for

my part I have good trust in our Lord God that
if I die to save the residue, that God will pardon
me.   Wherefore, to save them, I will be the first
to put my life in jeopardy."   When he had thus
said, every man worshipped him and divers kneeled
down at his feet with sore weeping and sore sighs.
Then another honest burgess rose and said, "I
will keep company with my gossip Eustace."   He
was called John Daire.   Then rose up Jacques of
Wisant, who was rich in goods and heritage; he
said also he would hold company with his two
cousins; likewise so did Peter Wisant, his brother.
And then rose two others and said they would do
the same.   Then they went and apparelled them
as the king desired.

Then the captain went with them to the gate;
there was great lamentation made of men, women,
and children at their departing.   Then the gate was
opened and he issued out with the six burgesses and
closed the gate again, for that they were between the
gate and the barriers.   Then he said to sir Walter
of Manny, "Sir, I deliver here to you as captain of
Calais, by the whole consent of all the people of the
town, these six burgesses.   And I swear to you truly
that they are to-day the most honourable, rich,
and most notable burgesses of all the town of Calais.
Wherefore, gentle knight, I beseech you pray the
king have mercy on them that they die not."   Quoth
sir Walter, "I can not say what the king will do, but
I shall do for them the best I can."   Then the
barriers were opened; the six burgesses went

CALAIS.

CALAIS VILLE MARITIME DE GRANDE ANTIQUITÉ ET IMPORTANCE

towards the king, and the captain entered again into the town. When sir Walter presented these burgesses to the king they kneeled down and held up their hands and said, "Gentle king, behold here we six, who were burgesses in Calais and great merchants, have brought to you the keys of the town and of the castle, and we submit ourselves clearly into your will and pleasure to save the residue of the people of Calais, who have suffered great pain. Sir, we beseech your grace to have mercy and pity on us through your high nobleness." Then all the earls and barons and others that were there wept for pity. Then the king looked felly on them, for greatly he hated the people of Calais for the great damages and dis-pleasures they had done him on the sea before. Then he commanded their heads to be stricken off. Then every man besought the king for mercy, but he would hear no man in that behalf. Then sir Walter of Manny said, "Ah! noble king, for God's sake refrain your wrath; you have the name of sovereign nobleness, therefore now do not a thing that should blemish your renown, nor give cause to some to speak of you any villany. Every man will say it is a great cruelty to put to death such honest persons, who by their own wills put themselves into your grace to save their company." Then the king turned away from him, and commanded to send for the hangmen, and said, "They of Calais have caused many of my men to be slain, wherefore these shall die in like wise." Then the queen, being great with child, kneeled down and sore weeping said, "Ah!

gentle sir, since I passed the sea in great peril I have desired nothing of you, therefore I now humbly pray you in honour of the Son of the Virgin Mary, and for the love of me, that you will take mercy of these six burgesses." The king beheld the queen, and stood still in thought a space, and then said, "Ah! dame, I would you had been now in some other place; you make such request of me that I cannot deny you. Wherefore I give them to you to do your pleasure with them." Then the queen caused them to be brought into her chamber, and made the halters to be taken from their necks, and caused them to be new-clothed, and gave them their dinner at their leisure. And then she gave each of them six nobles, and made them to be brought out of the host in safeguard and set at their liberty.

(In Sept. a truce was signed with Philip, and this was repeatedly renewed until 1355.)

1349.—Of the Black Death.

Knighton, 2599.

Then the grievous plague penetrated the seacoasts from Southampton, and came to Bristol, and there almost the whole strength of the town died, struck as it were by sudden death; for there were few who kept their beds more than three days, or two days, or half a day; and after this the fell death broke forth on every side with the course of the sun. There died at Leicester in the small parish of S. Leonard more than 380, in the parish of Holy Cross more than 400; in the parish of S. Margaret of Leicester more than 700 ; and so in each parish a great number. Then the bishop of Lincoln sent through the whole bishopric, and gave general power to all and every priest, both regular and secular, to hear confessions, and absolve with full and entire episcopal authority except in matters of debt, in which case the dying man, if he could, should pay the debt while he lived, or others should certainly fulfil that duty from his property after his death. Likewise, the pope granted full remission of all sins to whoever was absolved in peril of death, and granted that this power should last till next Easter, and everyone could choose a confessor at his will. In the same year there was a great plague of sheep everywhere in the realm, so that in one place there died in one pasturage more than 5,000 sheep, and so rotted that neither beast nor bird would touch them. And there were small prices for everything on account of the fear of death. For there were very few who cared about riches or anything else. For a man could have a horse, which before was worth 40s., for 6s. 8d., a fat ox for 4s., a cow for 12d., a heifer for 6d., a fat wether for 4d., a sheep for 3d., a lamb for 2d., a big pig for 5d., a stone of wool for 9d. Sheep and cattle went wandering over fields and through crops, and there was no one to go and drive or gather them, so that the number cannot be reckoned which perished in the ditches in every district, for lack of herdsmen; for there was such a lack of servants that no one knew what he ought to do.

In the following autumn no one could get a reaper for less than 8d. with his food, a mower for less than 12d. with his food. Wherefore many crops perished in the fields for want of some one to gather them; but in the pestilence year, as is above said of other things, there was such abundance of all kinds of corn that no one much troubled about it. The Scots, hearing of the cruel pestilence of the English, believed it had come to them from the avenging hand of God, and—as it was commonly reported in England—took for their oath when they wanted to swear, "By the foul death of England." But when the Scots, believing the English were under the shadow of the dread vengeance of God, came together in the forest of Selkirk, with purpose to invade the whole realm of England, the fell mortality came upon them, and the sudden and awful cruelty of death winnowed them, so that about 5,000 died in a short time. Then the rest, some feeble, some strong, determined to return home, but the English followed and overtook them and killed many of them.

Master Thomas of Bradwardine was consecrated by the pope archbishop of Canterbury, and when he returned to England he came to London, but within two days was dead. He was famous beyond all other clerks in the whole of Christendom, especially in theology, but likewise in the other liberal sciences. At the same time priests were in such poverty everywhere that many churches were widowed and lacking the divine offices, masses, mattins, vespers, sacraments, and other rites. A man could scarcely get a chaplain under £10 or 10 marks to minister to a church. And when a man could get a chaplain for 5 or 4 marks or even for two marks with his food when there was an abundance of priests before the pestilence, there was scarcely anyone now who was willing to accept a vicarage for £20 or 20 marks; but within a short time a very great multitude of those whose wives had died in the pestilence flocked into orders, of whom many were illiterate and little more than laymen, except so far as they knew how to read although they could not understand.

Meanwhile the king sent proclamation into all the counties that reapers and other labourers should not take more then they had been accustomed to take, under the penalty appointed by statute. But the labourers were so lifted up and obstinate that they would not listen to the king's command, but if anyone wished to have them he had to give them what they wanted, and either lose his fruit and crops, or satisfy the lofty and covetous wishes of the workmen. And when it was known to the king that they had not observed his command, and had given greater wages to the labourers, he levied heavy fines upon abbots, priors, knights, greater and lesser, and other great folk and small folk of the realm, of some 100s., of some 40s., of some 20s., from each according to what he could give. He took from each carucate * of the realm 20s., and, notwithstanding this, a fifteenth. And afterwards the king had many labourers arrested,

* A hundred acres.

and sent them to prison ; many withdrew themselves
and went into the forests and woods ; and those
who were taken were heavily fined.   Their ringleaders
were made to swear that they would not take daily
wages beyond the ancient custom, and then were freed
from prison.   And in like manner was done with the
other craftsmen in the boroughs and villages.   .   .
After the aforesaid pestilence, many buildings, great
and small, fell into ruins in every city, borough,
and village for lack of inhabitants, likewise many
villages and hamlets became desolate, not a house
being left in them, all having died who dwelt there ;
and it was probable that many such villages would
never be inhabited.   In the winter following there
was such a want of servants in work of all kinds,
that one would scarcely believe that in times past
there had been such a lack.   .   .   .   .   .   And so
all necessaries became so much dearer that what
in times past had been worth a penny, was then
worth 4d. or 5d.

Magnates and lesser lords of the realm who had
tenants made abatements of the rent in order that
the tenants should not go away on account of the
want of servants and the general dearness, some
half the rent, some more, some less, some for two
years, some for three, some for one year, according
as they could agree with them.   Likewise, those
who received of their tenants daywork throughout
the year, as is the practice with villeins, had to
give them more leisure, and remit such works, and
either entirely to free them, or give them an easier

tenure at a small rent, so that homes should not be everywhere irrecoverably ruined, and the land everywhere remain entirely uncultivated.

1349.—Of the death of abbot Michael of St. Alban's.

Chronicle of S. Albans, ii. 369.

(This example of the mortality caused by the Black Death is here given because it throws light on the condition of the most celebrated of English monasteries.)

He had brought much good to the monastery by his labour, when the pestilence came which destroyed almost the half of all flesh, and prevented him with untimely death; his life was cut off, as by a weaver's shears, when it seemed but beginning. He was touched by this common malady among the first of the monks struck by the fatal plague; and although on Sunday he began to feel the sickness of his body, yet moved by the solemnity of the festival and the memory of our Lord's humility, even before breakfast he solemnly celebrated a greater mass, and after mass with due humility and reverence washed the feet of his poor, and after the meal washed and kissed the feet of all the friars, and fulfilled all the duty of that day by himself without any help.

On the morrow, his sickness increasing, he betook himself to his bed, and like a true Catholic, having made a pure confession with contrition of heart, he received the last sacraments of unction; and so with grief and mourning drew out the time till the ninth day of Easter. On which day, while the convent was breakfasting, the hearts of all his monks were saddened by his departure. He had been carried from the false shadows of this world to the true light, from incessant labour to rest, from mourning to the ineffable joy of his Lord. Assuredly during the whole of his life, he was most pious, most compassionate, and, like as we are told of Moses, most mild.

There died at that time, besides those many who were lost at the cells (dependent priories), 47 monks of remarkable piety and learning, most of whom certainly had not their equals in virtue. This we believe was done for this purpose, that a man of angelic name and actions should not appear alone and without companions in the presence of the Judge, a man who his whole life had not ceased to multiply his Lord's talent, and had cleansed so much grain worthy to be carried into the Lord's granary.

But because there is no man on earth who does not sin, nor a son of man who does not offend, so, that he may not be believed entirely free from fault, to his negligence is it to be ascribed, that he pulled down and sold the beautiful hall made by the expense and care of his predecessor at his manor at Tydenhanger, to the no small inconvenience of his successors, and to the notable injury of the place. For this is the nature of almost all prelates who follow others, that they care little for the works of their predecessors, and either destroy their rich buildings or cease to visit them, caring more for other places that their fancy chooses. Yet the holy man must be forgiven, for although indeed he did commit this fault, yet he prepared and carried out innumerable benefits in comparison wherewith the error I have mentioned disappears, like a tiny drop of water thrown amid great flames.

1349.—Of the Flagellants.

Robert of Avesbury, p. 179.

In the year of our Lord 1349, about the feast of S. Michael, more than * men, having for the most part their origin in Zealand and Holland, came from Flanders to London, and sometimes in the church of S. Paul, sometimes in other places of the same city, twice a-day in the sight of the people, clad from thigh to ankle in linen cloth, the rest of the body bare, each having upon his head a cap marked with a red cross before and behind, each holding in the right hand a scourge with three cords, each (cord) having one knot, through the middle of some of which knots sharp nails were fixed, walked one after the other in procession with bare feet, and scourged themselves with these scourges on their bare and bleeding bodies, four of them singing in their language and four replying, like Litanies sung by Christians. In this procession they all thrice prostrated themselves to the ground, with their hands stretched in the shape of a cross, ever singing; and then finally some lay down and others stepped upon them and scourged them with their scourges, and this they did one after the other until the rite had been observed with all of them. Afterwards each put on his usual clothes,

* The number is wanting.

and bearing the caps on their heads and scourges
in their hands, they returned to their inns ; and did
like penance as was said, every night.

1349.—How sir Amery of Pavia, a Lombard, sold the town of Calais, whereof he was captain, to the lord Geoffrey Charny of France.

Froissart, ch. 150 (I. § 317).

All this season in the town of St. Omer was the
lord Geoffrey of Charny, who kept the frontiers there.
He bethought him how the Lombards naturally be
covetous ; wherefore he thought to assay to get the
town of Calais, whereof Amery of Pavia, a Lombard,
was captain. By reason of the truce they of St.
Omer might go to Calais, and they of Calais to St.
Omer, so that daily they resorted together to do
their merchandises.   Then sir Geoffrey secretly fell
into treaty with sir Amery of Pavia, so that he
promised to deliver into the Frenchmen's hands the
town and castle of Calais for twenty thousand
crowns. This was not done so secretly but that the
king of England had knowledge thereof ; then the
king sent for Amery of Pavia to come into England
to Westminster to speak with him, and so he came
over, for he thought that the king had not had
knowledge of the matter ; he thought he had done it
so secretly. When the king saw him he took him
apart and said, "Thou knowest well I have given
thee in keeping the thing in this world that I love
best, next my wife and children ; that is to say, the
town and castle of Calais, and thou hast sold it to

the Frenchmen, wherefore thou hast well deserved
to die." Then the Lombard knelt down and said,
"Ah, noble king, I cry your mercy. It is true that
ye say. But, sir, the bargain may well be broken,
for as yet I have received never a penny." The king
had loved well the Lombard, and said, "Amery, I
wish that thou go forward on thy bargain, and let me
have knowledge beforehand of the day thou appointest
to deliver up the town ; and upon this condition I
forgive thee thy trespass." . . Then sir Geoffrey of
Charny thought well to have Calais, and assembled
a certain number secretly, some five hundred spears.
There were but a few that knew what he purposed ;
I think he never made the French king of knowledge
thereof ; for if he had, I trow the king would not
have consented thereto, because of the truce. This
Lombard had appointed to deliver the castle the first
night of the new year, and sent word thereof by a
brother of his to the king of England.

**1350.—Of the battle at Calais between the king of
England, under the banner of sir Walter of
Manny, and sir Geoffrey of Charny and the
Frenchmen.**

Froissart, ch. 151 (1. §§ 318-9).

When the king of England knew the certain day
appointed, he departed out of England with three
hundred men of arms and six hundred archers,
and took shipping at Dover, and in the evening
arrived at Calais, so secretly that no man knew
thereof, and laid his men in bushments in the

chambers and towers within the castle. Then
the king said to sir Walter Manny, "I wish that
ye be chief of this enterprise, for I and my son
the prince will fight under your banner." The lord
Geoffrey of Charny, the last day of December at
night, departed from Arras and all his company,
and came near to Calais about the hour of midnight,
and sent two squires to the postern gate of the
castle of Calais, and there they found sir Amery
ready. Then they demanded of him if it were time
that the lord Geoffrey should come; and the
Lombard said, "Yes." Then sir Geoffrey sent
twelve knights with a hundred men of arms to go
and take possession of the castle of Calais, for
he thought well that if he might have the castle
he should soon get the town, seeing he had so great
a number of men with him and daily might have
more. And he delivered to the lord Odoart of
Renty twenty thousand crowns to pay the Lombard;
and sir Geoffrey remained still in the fields firmly,
with his banner before him. The Lombard let
down the bridge of the postern and suffered the
hundred men to enter peaceably, and sir Odoart
delivered at the postern twenty thousand crowns
in a bag to the Lombard, who said, "I trust here
be all, for I have no leisure now to count them,
for it will be day anon." Then he cast the bag
with crowns into a coffer, and said to the Frenchmen,
"Come on, sirs; ye shall enter into the donjon;
then shall you be sure to be lords of the castle."
They went thither, and he drew apart the bar, and

the gate opened. Within this tower was the king
of England with two hundred spears, who issued
out with their swords and axes in their hands, crying,
"Manny! Manny! to the rescue! What weeneth
the Frenchmen with so few men to win the castle
of Calais." Then the Frenchmen saw well that
defence could not avail them, and yielded themselves
prisoners, and they were put into the same tower
in prison. And the Englishmen issued out of the
castle into the town, and mounted on their horses,
for they had all the French prisoners' horses, and
rode to the Boulogne gate. There was sir Geoffrey
with his banner before him, for he had great desire
to be the first that should enter the town, and he
said to the knights that were about him, " Without
this Lombard open the gate shortly we are like to
die here for cold." " In the name of God, sir,"
said Pepin de Werre, " Lombards are malicious
people and subtle ; he is now looking on your crowns
to see if they be all good or not, and to reckon if he
have his whole sum or no." Therewith the king
of England and the prince, his son, were ready at
the gate, under the banner of sir Walter of Manny.
Then the great gate was set open, and they all
issued out. When the Frenchmen saw them issue
and heard them cry, " Manny to the rescue ! " they
knew well they were betrayed. Then sir Geoffrey
said to his company, " Sirs, if we fly we are clean
lost, so it were better to fight with a good heart."
The Englishmen heard these words and said, " By
Saint George, ye say truly, shame have he that

flieth." The Frenchmen alighted afoot and put
their horses from them and ordered themselves in
battle. When the king saw that, he stood still and
said, "Let us order ourselves in battle, for our
enemies will abide us." . . . .

Now let us speak of the king who was there
unknown of his enemies, under the banner of sir
Walter of Manny, and was afoot among his men to
seek his enemies, who stood together with their
spears, a five foot long. At the first meeting there
was a sore rencontre ; and the king lighted on the
lord Eustace of Ribeaumont, who was a strong and
hardy knight. There was a long fight between him
and the king, that it was joy to behold them ; at
last they were put asunder, for a great company
of both parties came the same way, and fought
there fiercely together. The Frenchmen did there
right valiantly, but especially the lord Eustace of
Ribeaumont, who struck the king the same day
two times on his knees, but finally the king himself
took him prisoner, and so he yielded his sword
to the king and said, "Sir knight, I yield me as
your prisoner," for he knew not then that it was
the king." And so the day was for the king of
England, and all that were there with sir Geoffrey
slain or taken.

**1350. — Of a chaplet of pearls that the king of
England gave to sir Eustace of Ribeaumont.**

Froissart, ch. 152 (1. § 320). *Jehan le Bel*, ch. 93.

When this battle was done the king returned again

to the castle of Calais, and caused all the prisoners
to be brought thither. Then the Frenchmen knew
well that the king had been there personally himself,
under the banner of sir Walter of Manny. The
king said he would give them all that night a supper
in the castle of Calais ; the hour of supper came and
the tables were covered. And the king and his
knights were there ready, every man in new apparel,
and the Frenchmen also were there and made good
cheer though they were prisoners. The king sat
down, and the lords and knights about him, right
honourably. The prince, the lords, and the knights
of England served the king at the first mess ; and at
the second they sat down at another table ; they
were all well served and at great leizure. Then
when supper was done and the tables taken away,
the king tarried still in the hall with his knights,
and with the Frenchmen, and he was bare headed
saving a chaplet of fine pearls that he wore on his
head. Then the king went from one to another of
the Frenchmen. And when he came to sir Geoffrey
of Charny, a little he changed his countenance, and
looked on him and said, " Sir Geoffrey, by reason I
should love you but a little, since you would steal by
night from me that thing which I have so dearly
bought, and which hath cost me so much gold.
I am right joyous and glad that I have taken you
with the proof. You would have a better market
than I have had when you thought to have had
Calais for twenty thousand crowns ; but God hath
holpen me, and you have failed of your purpose."

And therewith the king went from him, and he
gave never a word to answer. Then the king
came to sir Eustace of Ribeaumont and joyously
to him he said, "Sir Eustace, you are the knight
in the world that I have seen most valiantly assail
his enemies and defend himself, and I never found
knight that ever gave me so much ado, body to
body, as you have done this day. Wherefore
I give you the prize above all the knights of my
court by right sentence." Then the king took
the chaplet that was upon his head, being both
fair, goodly, and rich, and said: "Sir Eustace, I
give you this chaplet for the best doer in arms
in the battle past of either party, and I desire you
to bear it this year for the love of me. I know
well you are fresh and amorous, and oftentimes
are among ladies and damsels; say, wheresoever
you come, that I did give it you. And I quit you
from your prison and ransom, and you shall depart
to-morrow if it please you."

1350, Aug.—Of the naval battle and slaughter of the Spaniards upon the sea near Winchelsea.

Avesbury, 184.

(Contests between Biscayan and English fleets, due largely to
trade rivalries, had made the Channel unsafe; after this defeat,
the Biscay towns agreed to a twenty years' peace).

Our lord the king, considering how that about the
festival of All Saints a Spanish fleet, coming from the
sea towards Bordeaux, had captured in the mouth of
the Garonne several English ships laden with wine

to carry to England, and had killed all the English they found on board, determined to punish them with a like penalty, and frighten them from putting their hands any more to such crimes ; and so on the day of the Beheading of St. John the Baptist, in the year of our Lord 1350, the twenty-fourth year of his reign in England and the eleventh of his reign in France, having brought together a sufficient fleet at Sandwich, with many nobles, men-of-arms, and archers on board, he joined battle on the sea, near Winchelsea, with the Spaniards, who were sailing home with many war-ships from Flanders, and purposing to ravage the English shores. They fought bravely, but he overcame them ; and very many of the Spaniards in the twenty-four great galleys perished by the sword or flying arrow ; and all the twenty-four galleys, laden with much merchandise, especially various sorts of cloth bought in Flanders, were captured. But some, with wares in other ships, kept aloof from the battle and escaped, for none pursued them.

1351.—Of the coinage of groats and half-groats.

Walsingham, i. 275. *Murimuth, Continuatio*, 182.

In the year of grace one thousand three hundred and fifty-one, which was the twenty-fifth year of the reign of king Edward, from the conquest the third, William of Edyngdon, bishop of Winchester, treasurer of the kingdom, and a man of great prudence, who loved the good of the king more than that of the community, devised and caused to be coined a new

money, namely the groat and half-groat; but these
were of less weight than the like sum of sterling.
This was afterwards the cause that food and merchandise became dearer throughout the whole of England.
Workmen, craftsmen, and servants became accordingly more cunning and fraudulent than ever. To
provide against their cunning and pride, wickedness
and avarice, statutes were afterwards ordained by the
parliament at Westminster in the 28th and 35th years
of the reign of Edward the third from the conquest;
but they were of little or no service to the Commons.

1351, Feb.—Statute of Provisors.

25 *Edw. III., Statute* 4. *(Statutes of the Realm,* ed. 1810, i. 316.*)*

(This most important statute was an attempt to put an end to
the papal encroachments on free election to bishoprics, and on
private rights of patronage. In spite of frequent evasions, it
had the effect of lessening the evil complained of.)

.   .   .   . Now it is shewed to our lord the king
in this present parliament holden at Westminster, at
the Octave of the Purification of our Lady, the
five-and-twentieth year of his reign of England
and of France the twelfth, by the grievous complaints
of all the commons of his realm, that the grievances
and mischiefs aforesaid do daily abound, to the
greater damage and destruction of all his realm
of England, more than ever were before, viz., that
now or late the bishop of Rome, by procurement
of clerks or otherwise, hath reserved and doth daily
reserve to his collation, generally and especially
as well archbishopricks, bishopricks, abbeys and

priories, as all other dignities and other benefices
in England, which be of the advowry of * people
of Holy Church, and give the same as well to
aliens as to denizens, and taketh of all such benefices
the first fruits, and many other profits; and a great
part of the treasure of the said realm is carried
away and dispended out of the realm, by the
purchasers of such benefices and graces aforesaid;
and also by such privy reservations many clerks
advanced in this realm by their true patrons, which
have peaceably holden their advancements by long
time be suddenly put out; whereupon the said
commons have prayed our said lord the king, that
since the right of the crown of England and the
law of the said realm is such that, upon the mischiefs
and damages which happen to his realm, he ought
and is bound by his oath, with the accord of his
people in parliament, thereof to make remedy and
law, in removing the mischiefs and damages which
thereof ensue, it may please him thereupon to ordain
remedy. Our lord the king . . . . . by the
assent of all the great men and commonality of
the said realm, to the honour of God and profit
of the said Church of England and of all his realm
hath ordered and established, that the free elections
of archbishops, bishops, and all other dignities and
benefices elective in England, shall hold from
henceforth in the manner as they were granted by
the king's progenitors, and the ancestors of other
lords, founders of the said dignities and other

* In the gift of.

benefices. And that all prelates and other people of Holy Church, which have advowsons of any benefices of the king's gift, or of any of his progenitors, or of other lords and donors, to do divine services and other charges thereof ordained, shall have their collations and presentments freely to the same, in the manner as they were enfeoffed by their donors.

1352.—Statute of Treasons.

25 *Edward III. Stat.* 5, *c.* 2. (*Statutes of the Realm*, i. 319).

(This was the first definition by statute of the acts constituting treason, and it became the basis of all subsequent legislation and judicial decision.)

Item, whereas divers opinions have been before this time in what case treason shall be said and in what not; the king, at the request of the lords and of the commons, hath made a declaration in the manner as hereafter followeth, that is to say, when a man doth compass or imagine the death of our lord the king, or of our lady his queen, or of their eldest son and heir; or if a man do violate the king's consort, or the king's eldest daughter unmarried, or the wife of the king's eldest son and heir; or if a man do levy war against our lord the king in his realm, or be adherent to the king's enemies in his realm, giving to them aid and comfort in the realm or elsewhere, and thereof be proveably attainted of open deed by the people of their condition; and if a man counterfeit the king's great or privy seal or his money; and if a man bring false money into this realm counterfeit to the money of England, . . . knowing the money to be false, to merchandise or make payment in deceit of our said lord the king or of his people ; and if a man slay the chancellor, treasurer, or the king's justices of the one bench or the other, justices in eyre or justices of assize, and all other justices assigned to hear or determine, being in their places, doing their offices. And it is to be understood that, in the cases above rehearsed, that ought to be judged treason which extends to our lord the king and his royal majesty ; and of such treason the forfeiture of the escheats pertains to our sovereign lord, as well of the lands and tenements holden of others as of himself. And moreover there is another manner of treason, that is to say, when a servant slayeth his master or a wife her husband, or when a man secular or religious slayeth his prelate to whom he oweth faith and obedience ; and of such treason the escheats ought to pertain to every lord of his own fee. And because that many like cases of treason may happen in time to come which a man cannot think nor declare at this present time, it is accorded that if any other case, supposed treason, which is not above specified, doth happen before any justices, the justices shall tarry without any going to judgment of the treason till the cause be showed before the king and his parliament, and it be declared whether it ought to be judged treason or other felony.

1353.—A statute against annullers of judgments of the king's court (commonly called the statute of Præmunire).

27 *Edw. III., Stat.* 1, *cap.* 1 (*Statutes*, i. 329).

(This, like the statute of Provisors, was a defensive measure against Rome, and was designed to prevent encroachments on the jurisdiction of the English courts. The act known later as the statute of Præmunire was a confirmation and completion of this, and was passed in 1393.)

Our lord the king, by the assent and prayer of the great men and the commons of the realm of England, at his great council holden at Westminster, the Monday next after the feast of Saint Matthew the Apostle, the twenty-seventh year of his reign of England, and of France the fourteenth, in amendment of his said realm, and maintenance of the laws and usages, hath ordained and stablished these things under written.

First, because it is shewed to our lord the king, by the grievous and clamorous complaints of the great men and commons aforesaid, how that divers of the people be and have been drawn out of the realm to answer of things, whereof the cognisance pertaineth to the king's court, and also that the judgments given in the same court be impeached in another court, in prejudice and disherison of our lord the king and of his crown and of all the people of his said realm and to the undoing and destruction of the common law of the same realm at all times used : whereupon, good deliberation had with the great men and others of his said council, it is assented and accorded by our lord the king and the great men and commons aforesaid, that all the people of the king's ligeance, of what condition they be, which shall draw any out of the realm in plea whereof the cognizance pertaineth to the king's court, or of things whereof judgments be given in the king's court, or which do sue in any other court, to defeat or impeach the judgments given in the king's court, shall have a day, containing the space of two months, by warning to be made to them in the place where the possessions be which be in debate, or otherwise where they have lands or other possessions, by the sheriffs or other the king's ministers, to appear before the king and his council, or in his chancery, or before the king's justices in his places of the one bench or the other, or before other the king's justices which to the same shall be deputed, to answer in their proper persons to the king of the contempt done in this behalf. And if they come not at the said day in their proper persons to be at the law, they, their procurators, attornies, executors, notaries, and maintainors shall from that day forth be put out of the king's protection, and their lands, goods, and chattels forfeit to the king, and their bodies, wheresoever they may be found, shall be taken and imprisoned, and ransomed at the king's will; and upon the same a writ shall be made to take them by their bodies, and to seize their lands, goods, and possessions, into the king's hands; and if it be returned, that they be not found, they shall be . . . . . . outlawed.

**1351, March 27.—How the lord Robert of Beau-
manoir went about to defy the captain of Ploërmel who had to name Bramborough, and how
there was a sore battle of thirty against thirty.**

Froissart (I. §§ 335-7).

(In spite of the truce between the English and French kings,
the war continued in Brittany; Charles of Blois had been taken
prisoner in 1347, and sent to join David Bruce in the Tower of
London, but his wife gallantly continued the struggle. Its most
celebrated episode was the Tourney of Ploërmel.)

In this same season there took place in Brittany a
very great deed of arms that ought never to be
forgotten, but rather ought to be put forward to
encourage all young squires, and to give them an
example. And that you may the better understand
the matter you must know that there were wars
continually between the parties of the two ladies
Joan of Montfort and Joan of Blois, because that
the lord Charles of Blois was imprisoned. And the
parties of these same ladies warred on each other by
means of their garrisons, which kept themselves
within their castles and their strong towns both on
the one side and on the other.

It chanced one day that the lord Robert of Beaumanoir, a right valiant knight and of the most high
lineage in Brittany, who was seneschal of the castle
which has to name the castle Josselin, and who had
with him a goodly company of men-of-arms of his
own lineage and others who were mercenaries,
came before the town and the castle of Ploërmel.
Its captain was a man named Bramborough, and he

had with him a great company of mercenaries, German, English, and Breton, who were of the party of the countess of Montfort. And this same lord Robert with his company ran before the barriers, and would gladly have seen those within sally forth, but not one stirred. When sir Robert saw this, he approached yet a little nearer and called to the captain. And he came before the gate to speak with the said sir Robert, on the safe assurance on the one hand and on the other.

"Bramborough," said sir Robert, "are there no men of arms within your walls, either you or other two or three, who would joust with lances against other three on our party for the love of their friends?"

Bramborough answered and said, "Their friends would never wish that they should be evilly killed in a single joust, for that would be a chance of fortune too soon over, and would win them the name of foolhardiness and folly, rather than bring them renown. But I will tell you what we will do, an it please you. You shall take twenty or thirty of your companions from your garrison, and I will take as many from mine. And let us go to a fair field, where none shall hinder or trouble us, and command our companions, on pain of hanging, on the one side and on the other, and also all those who stand and watch us, that none shall give aid or comfort to any of the combatants. And there straitly in that place let us prove ourselves and do such things that in the time to come men shall speak of us in halls and in palaces, in public places and in all other parts of the world. And let the renown and the good-luck be to those to whom God shall award it."

"By my troth," said sir Robert of Beaumanoir, "I accord me thereunto, and right valiantly do you now speak. Therefore, be you thirty, and we also will be thirty, and this I vow on my faith."

"And this I also on my part vow," said Bramborough, "for there will thus be gained more honour, to him who there bears himself bravely than at a single joust."

Thus was the matter settled and sworn to ; and the day agreed on was the Wednesday following. In the meantime each one chose those thirty followers that seemed good to him, and all these sixty looked well to their armour that all might be right and in good order.

When the day came Bramborough's thirty companions heard mass ; then armed themselves and went to the place where the battle was to be, and there alighted on foot ; and they straitly forbad all those who were there that they should come between them for whatever chance or peril they might see befall to their companions. And thus likewise did the thirty companions of the lord Robert of Beaumanoir. And these thirty companions, that we call the English, awaited for a great space those others that we call the French. When the thirty Frenchmen were come, they alighted from their horses and gave to their followers the same commandment that the English knights had given. Each side agreed that

five of them should remain on horseback at the
entrance of the place, and that the other twenty-five
should alight. And when they were each before the
other, the whole sixty held parley together for a short
space; then they drew back on the one side and on
the other, and made all their followers withdraw to a
greater distance. Then one of them made a sign,
and forthwith they ran forward, and fiercely they
fought in the press, and nobly they succoured each
the other, where they saw their companions in
great straits. And shortly after that they were
gathered together, was one of the French party
slain, but for all that the others never ceased the
battle, but bore themselves as valiantly on the one
part and on the other, as if they all had been Rolands
and Olivers. I cannot say of a truth that they on
this hand maintained themselves the better, or that
they on that hand achieved greater things, nor have
I heard either party prized before the other; but
they fought so long that one and all lost strength
and breath and power altogether. And they were
forced to stop and take rest; and by agreement they
rested, the one on this side and the other on that,
and made truce until such time as they should be
rested, and the first to arise was to call on the other
party.

And of the Frenchmen there were slain four, and
of the Englishmen two. Thus they rested on both
sides for a long space, and drank wine that was
brought to them in bottles, rebuckled their disordered armour, and dressed their wounds. When

they were thus refreshed, the first party which arose
made a sign and called on the other. Then began
as before a sore and fierce battle which lasted a
long while. They fought with the short swords of
Bordeaux, strong and sharp, and with lances and
daggers, and others with axes, and they gave each
other marvellous great blows, and one and all threw
themselves into the battle, and smote each other
without sparing. You may well believe they did
right noble deeds of arms man for man, body to
body, and hand to hand. There has never been
heard tell of such deeds for this hundred years past.
Thus they fought together like good champions, and
maintained this second encounter right valiantly,
but finally the English were worsted. For thus have
I heard it related how that one of the Frenchmen
who was on horseback broke and scattered them so
fiercely that Bramborough, their captain, and eight
of their companions were there slain ; and the others
yielded themselves prisoners when they saw how
their defence would not aid them, for they could not
and would not fly. And the same lord Robert and
his companions who were yet alive took them, and
led them to the castle Josselin as their prisoners,
and afterwards put them to ransom courteously when
that they were all cured of their hurts ; for there
were none who were not sore wounded, Frenchmen
no less than Englishmen.

And since that time I have seen sitting at the table
of Charles king of France a Breton knight, sir Evan
of Charuel who had been there ; and he had his face

so cut about and hacked that it plainly showed how
that the encounter had been nobly fought. And in
many places was this adventure related and recorded,
and some thought it prowess and others foolhardiness.

1351.—The Tourney of Ploërmel.

Translated from a French poem of the 14th century; in Buchon,
Froissart, xiv., 303 (Coll. des Chronique, xxiv.)

Oh! hearken to my tale, ye lords and knights of
      chivalry,
Both bannerets and bachelors and men of high degree,
Let abbots eke and bishops hear and men of holy
      mind,
Heralds and wandering minstrels, and all companions
      kind,
Gentle and simple folk, in whatsoever land ye dwell,
Give heed unto this brave romance, that we to you
      would tell.
True is the tale and worthy, right worthy to be told,
How thirty English champions in war like lions bold,
Fought on a day with thirty knights of Breton
      lineage.

.   .   .   .

Ere that the lord Dagorne was dead and knew this
      life no more,
(At Auril fell the baron the castle walls before,
—— On all such lords of Brittany and their com-
      panions brave
May our just God have mercy who knows to sain and
      save!)

While yet this lord was living, he did all folk to
    know,
That no more should the village folk, the men who
    reap and sow,
Be captured of the Englishmen, and vexed with spear
    and sword ;
But, when he died, his comrades heeded no more his
    word,
For Bramborough clave unto him, to his allegiance
    true,
And by St. Thomas swore he a vengeful deed to do.
The Breton folk he harried and took the country
    side,
And Poetinel he plundered till her folk for pity cried.
All through the coasts of Brittany he wrought his evil
    way,
Up to the time that God had doomed to be his
    closing day ;
But at last the good lord Beaumanoir, whom all men
    loved to name,
The wise lord John of Beaumanoir, whose valour
    wrought him fame,
To parley with the Englishmen in happy hour he
    went,
And saw their wretched captives, and 'gan their woe
    lament.
For one was vexed with fetters, and another dragged
    a chain,
And another in the stocks was bound, and some
    were pent in pain,
And all were bound together with thongs in twos and
    threes,

Like to the cows and oxen men barter as they please.
When Beaumanoir beheld them, deep in his heart he
    sighed,
And unto Bramborough spake he, right noble in his
    pride;
"Oh knights of English chivalry, to right ye do foul
    scorn
In harrying the husbandmen, the men who sow the
    corn,
Who win for us our meat and wine where they them-
    selves did sow.
Ah, had we not the husbandmen, too well we soon
    should know
The toil of working in the field, all noble though we
    be,
The work of threshing, hoeing, and bearing poverty.
To men unused like us to this no little toil it were.
Let these then rest henceforward, who have too
    much to bear,
Nor let the will of brave Dagorne be cast aside so
    soon."

    (A combat is agreed upon, as described by Froissart in the
previous extract.)

Now will I tell of Bramborough and all the deeds
    he wrought,
His thirty men he gathered, and them hath fairly
    brought
Straight to the field appointed, in gallant wise and gay,
And then to all his company these noble truths 'gan say,
"Well have I conned my magic, my books of mystery,
And on this day doth Merlin foretell us victory.

Henceforth o'er France and Brittany, if I the truth
    can know,
Shall Edward have the governance ; for fate will
    have it so."

    .   .   .   .

Then spake he unto Beaumanoir, "Look not for
    ruth from me ;
My mind is fixed before my love this day to carry
    thee.
This day I vow to lead thee a captive to her bower."
And Beaumanoir cried back to him, "Deemest thou
    that will is power ?
Lo ! I and all my company know our intent aright,
And if the Lord of Glory aid and Mary lend us
    might,
If good St. Yvës help us, in whom our trust we place,
Mock not thyself with idle hopes, but cast the die
    apace.
The hazard is against thee, and short thy life shall be."
And Alain, lord of Carromois, heard too, and loud
    cried he,
" Bramboro', thou villain traitor ! hop'st thou that
    this shall be ?
Think'st thou that men like Beaumanoir can yield
    to men like thee ?
For him upon my body forthwith I thee defy,
And now before my edged blade I deem that thou
    shalt die."
Straightway the lord of Carromois hath smitten him
    with might

And sorely stabbed him with his lance, the spearhead
    keen and bright,
Right through his face the spearhead went, for all
    men round to see,
And right within his brain-pan stuck and pierced
    him grievously.
Then Alain thrust the spear from him and laid bold
    Bramborough low ;
But Bramborough leapt to gain his feet and thought
    to reach his foe,
Then Geoffrey lord of Borës dealt him a blow amain
And pierced him with his spearhead and laid him
    low again,
Till in the dust bold Bramborough fell with a crash
    and died.
Then to the lord of Beaumanoir brave Geoffrey gladly
    cried,
"Where art thou ? see'st this vengeance ? see'st thou
    who here lies slain ? "
And Beaumanoir hath heard him and answered back
    again,
"Now 'tis the time for prowess ! on to the combat
    go !
On, lords, to war with others and leave the dead man
    low."
Then well saw all the Englishmen, how Bramborough
    there was dead,
And all their pride fell from them, and all their
    boasting fled.
Then to his friends cried Croucart, a German fell
    in fight,

"Lords, wot ye well the truth this day and know
　　　your case aright,
Bramborough, who led us hither with bitter mockery,
Has mocked us, and his trusted books of Merlin's
　　　mystery
Have not been worth a penny to him for all his trust.
Dead on his back with gaping throat he lieth in the
　　　dust.
Now act we all like wise men, like comrades brave
　　　and stout,
Stand back to back in order close, and fight the
　　　battle out.
Let all who come against us find death or sudden
　　　fear."

　　·　　·　　·　　·　　·　　·　　·　　·

Then fiercely went the battle and victory came slow,
As still the dreadful combat went swaying to and fro.
　　·　　·　　·　　·　　·　　·　　·
And hot the sun shone over them, and every man did
　　　sweat,
With sweat and blood beneath their feet the earth
　　　itself grew wet.
It chanced on this fair Saturday that Beaumanoir
　　　kept fast,
And evil grew his thirst to him; he cried for drink
　　　at last,
And Geoffrey, lord of Borës, heard him, and answered
　　　"Nay,
Drink of thy blood, lord Beaumanoir; thy thirst
　　　thyself canst stay.

This day we win great glory, no man shall lack his
　　fame ;
Our great renown of valour shall never bring us
　　blame."
Then did the lord of Beaumanoir take courage and
　　delight,
And all his thirst passed from him in the joy and
　　breath of fight.
And from each side the battles met fiercely face to
　　face,
And men fell dead or wounded ; few living left that
　　place.　　　　　　　　　•

1354.—How the duke of Lancaster in vain treated for peace at Avignon.

Knighton, 2607.

(Philip VI. of France had died in 1350, and his eldest son
John had succeeded him. In spite of the war in Brittany,
the truce was several times renewed; and in 1354 the new
pope, Innocent VI., seemed likely to bring about peace. A
conference of ambassadors met at Guines near Calais, and
Edward offered to give up his claim to the French throne if
Guienne were given him in full sovereignty. The treaty was
to be completed at Avignon.)

Then were sent to Avignon to the pope to treat
for peace the duke of Lancaster, the earl of Arundel,
the bishop of Norwich, and many magnates. But
the ambassadors of France, to wit the duke of
Bourbon, the earl of Armagnac, and the rest, dis-
avowed all the articles to which they had consented
and agreed at Calais, and would accept no peace except
on their own terms, declaring that they were ready

and able to defend their land against the English,
world without end ; and so they parted. For the
French demanded, first, that the king of England
should give up the arms of France ; secondly, that
the king of England should do homage to the king
of France for Gascony. The duke of Lancaster
replied that the arms of France, which he bore by
the counsel of his liege men of France, he would not
give up for any man living. Also the king of England would not do homage to a man to whom he
claimed to be superior by hereditary right from his
mother. But if they would propose any other reasonable terms of peace, the king of England loved
peace so much that he would accept them.

Henry duke of Lancaster, having with him the
the earl of Arundel and the rest, had arrived at
Avignon on Christmas Eve, with two hundred horses,
of which thirty-two were covered with harness of
mail, and he remained there for six weeks with great
honour. Indeed, when he had been approaching the
city, bishops, nobles, citizens, and commons had
come out to meet him to the number of two thousand
horsemen ; and there was such a crowd that from
the third hour of the day to vespers they could
scarce pass over the city bridge. When he had
entered the city, he had gone straightway to the
palace of the pope. And, arriving there, he dis-
mounted and, entering in, saluted the pope with
due reverence, as he knew well how to do, and,
after brief converse, passed to his lodging. The
joys of feasting and drinking were always ready,

so long as he stayed there, for all who wished to
come and refresh themselves ; and everything was
so carefully provided that all the court was astonished ;
—before his arrival, a hundred casks of wine had
been got ready in his cellar. He showed such
courtesy to all, especially to the pope and the
cardinals, that they said the wide world had not
his fellow. After he had left the papal court, the
French laid ambush for him to take him, but by
the help of God he escaped many snares and came
to England with great honour.

1354.—Of the trouble between the Oxford scholars and laity.

Avesbury, 197.

On the festival of S. Scolastica the Virgin a quarrel
began in a tavern at Oxford between a scholar and
the taverner about a quart of wine, and the scholar
after pouring the wine over the taverner broke his
head with the quart pot. Whereupon there arose a
great conflict between the scholars of the university
and the laymen of the town of Oxford, in which
many laymen were wounded and about twenty were
slain ; and some of the scholars also were severely
wounded ; and this conflict went on at intervals for
two days. On the second day the monks made a
solemn procession supplicating for peace. But still
the conflict went on ; and a young scholar pursued by
laymen ran for safety to a monk who was with due
humility bearing the Body of Christ in the procession,
hoping that he would be saved by their reverence
for the Body ; but in vain, for the laymen cruelly

attacked the innocent youth and mortally wounded him.   Later in the same day the riot stopped, by the grace of God, and peace was publicly proclaimed between the parties.   But next morning the laymen from the villages around Oxford, confederate with the laymen of that town, came in hostile array and great power into the town of Oxford with a black banner before them.   They drove the scholars to their inns, broke about twenty doors of scholars' houses, went into the private rooms in the inns and killed, so it was said, many scholars, cut their books about with knives and axes, and carried off much of their property.   Thus, alas! the university was dissolved, and no one became bachelor or master in dialectic art ; all the scholars went home, except only the scholars of Merton Hall and of other like halls, and a few others.

On the first Sunday in Lent the king held a great feast and made a great tournament at Woodstock, because just then the queen was churched after the birth of her son Thomas, who was born there, and was held over the sacred font by Thomas, bishop of Durham.   The bishop of Lincoln receiving full information of the troubles at Oxford, inhibited all the rectors and other priests over the whole of Oxford from celebrating mass or other divine offices in the presence of any layman of the town ; and this interdict was not removed for more than a year.   The king also sent his justices to the town, and many laymen and clergy also were conducted before them.   Four of the more important burgesses of the town were indicted, and by royal command arrested, and taken off to the Tower of London, and there remained in prison. And in the great council held at Westminster after Easter, in the year 1355, our lord the king took into his hands the whole quarrel between the scholars and laity of Oxford, and, saving all rights, pardoned certain scholars for all the faults they had committed, and gave orders by writs to all the sheriffs of England that this should be publicly proclaimed ; and accordingly in summer the university of Oxford flourished again in all the faculties. For some took their degrees in the dialectic art, some in theology, some in civil law, some in canon law, and some in both civil and canon. And our lord the king granted the complete supervision of the assize of bread, ale, and wine, and all. victuals to the chancellor of the university, excluding the mayor entirely. The corporation paid as a fine to the university two hundred and fifty pounds sterling, without detriment to individual suits.

1355.—How the prince of Wales crossed to Gascony.
Avesbury, 201.

It was determined in the council at Westminster that the lord Edward, the prince of Wales, who was in the 24th year of his age, should cross to Gascony, and should have with him the earls of Warwick, Suffolk, Salisbury, and Oxford, with a thousand men of arms, two thousand archers, and a great number of Welsh. Soon afterwards the prince journeyed from London to Plymouth, where the navy for the passage was gathering, and there stayed, because the winds were contrary, until the festival of the Nativity of the Blessed Mary; and then the prince, with some three hundred ships and many more men than had been ordained, set sail with a favorable wind from the north, and safely and quickly passed to Gascony, where he was received by the Gascons with great joy, and there performed great deeds, as will appear later.

1355.—How the duke of Lancaster tarried on the sea, and of the treason plotted by the king of Navarre.

Avesbury, 202.

At the same time the king of England caused his forty great ships to be prepared at Rotherhithe

in the Thames with food for a quarter of a year;
each of these vessels bore the banners of the lord
Henry duke of Lancaster, and were filled with picked
men at arms and archers; but they took no horses
with them. The whole was commanded by the said
duke, and he had with him two sons of the king,
namely, the lord Lionel of Antwerp and John of
Gaunt, the elder being then sixteen, as well as the
earls of Northampton, of March, and of Stafford.
On the tenth of July they began to sail and got
to Greenwich. There and at Sandwich they tarried
until the festival of the Assumption, the wind being
constantly from the west or the east, so that they
could not sail. With difficulty they got as far as
Winchelsey, and afterwards to the Isle of Wight.
Meanwhile the king was on board with the duke,
in order to negotiate with the ambassadors of the
king of Navarre,* who frequently came across to
him. The fleet were in this condition when it was
rumoured that the duke intended to cross to
Normandy, where the king of Navarre promised
to receive him in his castle of Cherbourg. For
a quarrel had arisen between the king of Navarre
and John king of France, wherefore the former
turned from John, and sent promises to the king
of England that he would join him with all his
power. But bye-and-bye the duke of Lancaster
learnt through spies that the king of Navarre had
made peace with the king of France, and that the
latter plotted to entrap the king of England and

* See *Appendix*.

the duke.   And this was proved by the evidence
of fact.

For near the castle on the sea coast there lay
in ambush several thousand men of arms, some
French and others German mercenaries, awaiting
the duke's arrival.   So when he heard of the
treachery which was thus plotted, the duke, since his
force was small in comparison with the enemy, and
he had no cavalry, returned into England, his plan
having been frustrated completely.

1355.—How the king of England crossed to Calais and laid waste a great part of Picardy.

Avesbury, 204.

On the Saturday after the feast of the Nativity of
the Blessed Virgin Mary, the king caused proclamation to be made in the city of London that all nobles,
men of arms, and archers should be ready at Sandwich on S. Michael's day, to cross with him to Calais.
For he had heard that king John of France had prepared a great army to fight with him as soon as he
should come into those parts.   So about that time
the lord Thomas, bishop of Durham, the lord of
Percy, and the other nobles of the north, made a
truce with the Scots to last till the day of the Nativity
of S. John next following ; and then the said lords
came to the king at Sandwich, and crossed with him.
The king had with him his two sons, the lord Lionel
of Antwerp, and the lord John of Ghent, as well as the
lord Henry Duke of Lancaster, and the earls of
Northampton, March, and Stafford.   At Calais also

he found a thousand good men of arms, mercenaries from Flanders, Brabant, and Germany. And the Londoners had sent to the king twenty-five men of arms, and a body of five hundred archers, at their own expense. So altogether the king had more than three thousand men of arms, a great number of armed men, about two thousand mounted archers, as well as very many archers on foot. On the second of November the king left Calais with his army, and marched towards St. Omer, laying waste all the country as he passed. When John king of France, who was near St. Omer with a strong army, heard this he sent a certain knight, named sir Boucicault,—who had been captured in Gascony and had long been a prisoner in the hands of the king of England, but had just been ransomed,—to speak with the king of England and observe his army. And when he met the king, and with his permission had observed the three divisions of the English so nobly ordered, and composed of such warlike and wonderfully brave men, he was surprised that the king of England had such a large force with him, considering that the prince of Wales had also so great an army in Gascony. So he returned to king John and told him what he had seen. Then king John was sore troubled, and feared to meet the noble king of England face to face, but rather sought subterfuges; and therefore turned round and marched off, as far in front of the king of England as he could, destroying all provisions on the way that the English should not use them. The king of England pursued the retreating foe for some days, finding however very little food; and the scarcity of drink was such that for three days the greater part of the English army had nothing to drink but water.. And when the king had passed Hesdin towards Amiens, seeing the cowardice of the enemy, and that they would not give battle. . . he returned through more fruitful lands to Boulogne, and thence returned to Calais, having been away ten days. Next day the constable of France and other Frenchmen came to Calais and offered battle for the next Tuesday. To whom the English lords replied at the order of the king, that the king wanted as much as possible to avoid the shedding of Christian blood, and therefore wished to meet his adversary, body to body, in his own cause, on condition that their right to the kingdom of France should be decided by battle between the two alone; or if his adversary was unwilling to fight by himself, then each should add to himself his eldest son; and if this were not enough, each should take two, three, or four noble knights nearest in blood to themselves and their sons; and that the conquered should yield his claims to the conqueror. These offers the Frenchmen totally rejected, and promised battle on the Tuesday.

(The Frenchmen would not accept an earlier day, nor pledge themselves to the good faith of John : Tuesday was at last agreed upon, but John did not appear).

Whereupon Edward gave each of the foreign mercenaries over, and above the promised pay, presents in proportion to their rank, and returned to England much praised.

1355.—Capture of Berwick by the Scots.

Avesbury, 209-10.

(In 1354 the conditions upon which king David Bruce should be free had been arranged, but before they could be carried out, French men and money appeared in Scotland and encouraged the national party to renew the struggle.)

While the events above told were taking place abroad, the Scots came secretly to the town of Berwick with great force, on the sixth of November, and entered the town at sunrise by stealth and unobserved by the garrison. Two or three English who tried to resist were slain ; the whole town and all that it contained were captured ; save that some took refuge in the castle and held it.

(Edward on his return held a parliament, which granted him large supplies.)

On S. Andrew's day (Nov. 30), parliament being at an end, our noble lord the king hastened towards Scotland, and kept Christmas at Newcastle-on-Tyne ; meanwhile causing a great army to be gathered for the recovery of Berwick.

1355.—Of the terrible and wonderful expedition of the prince of Wales from Bordeaux to Narbonne.

Avesbury, 210.

While the king of England was in Northumberland preparing to enter Scotland, letters came to London from the lord Edward, his eldest son, who was then warring in Gascony, and also other letters from the lord John of Wingfield, knight, who was then and had long been as it were the leader and chief councillor of the prince, directed to the lord bishop of Winchester, treasurer of the king, saying how the prince had harried all the lands not yet under the allegiance of the king of England from the city of Bordeaux to the city of Narbonne, which is near the Greek sea.* He had taken by assault about five hundred country towns, and many great cities and walled towns, taking infinite spoil, and laying the country waste by fire for eight weeks. The city of Narbonne was captured, all but the castle; and when the men of Montpellier heard this, they feared lest they should suffer the same fate, and therefore had all the houses in the suburbs taken down and the materials carried into the city. The scholars of the university there, and even the friars, and many others who lived in the suburbs, as well as a great number from the country around, betook themselves in terror to Avignon, with such property as they could carry, that they might be under the protection of the pope. Our lord the pope, not thinking himself safe, caused all the gates of his palace to be secured with iron. The pope's marshal went out to meet the prince with more than five hundred men of arms, some Provençals and some from the retinues of the lord cardinals, but fifty of his men were slain, the marshal himself was captured, and set to ransom for 50,000 shield-florins, bringing back scarcely more than 80 of his men. *So they were shrunk in the wetting!* After destroying Narbonne, the prince of Wales heard that the earl of Armagnac, the constable of France, the marshal of Clermont,

* The Mediterranean.

and the prince of Orange, with other magnates, had
gathered an innumerable force against him, and were
coming against him to join battle, and therefore he
turned to meet them. Whereupon the Frenchmen
were struck with terror, and dared not to stand in his
way, and fled into the mountains and other safe places
where they could not be attacked.

1356.—Burnt Candlemas.

Avesbury, 235.

(The Scotch in Berwick had quickly capitulated. Edward now
thought it possible to gain the direct sovereignty of Scotland, and
caused Edward Balliol to formally make over to him all his
rights to the throne.)

On Jan. 27 the lord Edward, king of England,
the kingdom and crown of Scotland having been thus
transferred to him at Roxburgh, began to ride forward
in his new kingdom of Scotland, having with him
three thousand men of arms, and ten thousand armed
men, more than ten thousand archers on horseback,
and as many more on foot, carrying among other
standards the royal banner of Scotland. Then
William Douglas, a lord very rich in those parts,
came to the king with words of peace, and craftily
begged for a truce of ten days, wherein he might
speak to the other nobles of the kingdom of Scotland,
and win them over to the allegiance of the new
king of Scotland. And the king, being perfect in
charity and believing everything, granted him the
truce. But, during the ten days, the said William and the
other lords of those parts around the Scotch sea had

as much of their property as they could carried to the
castles and other secret subterranean places, and then
when the ten days were over, they fled from the face
of the king and betook themselves to hiding-places
in the woods and marshes. Then the king, seeing
that he was greatly deceived by William Douglas,
ravaged aud burnt all his lands and those of other
lords as far as the Scotch sea, so that nothing that
could be taken remained unburnt. But they had
very little food, and many ships coming from
England to the king with food were so horribly
tost by the tempests of the sea that some of them
were lost, others were driven by the winds to various
English ports, and some were borne to foreign parts.
So, as food failed them, our lord the king returned
to England, being for the time frustrated in his
purpose.

1356.—The night before Poitiers.

Froissart, ch. 159 (1. § 377.)

(In the summer the duke of Lancaster crossed to La Hogue,
and ravaged Normandy; but being met by the French king with a
superior force he turned aside into Brittany. On July 6, the
prince of Wales left Bordeaux with a small army and marched
north, hoping to join Lancaster. King John thereupon turned
south and near Poitiers caught up the prince who was returning
on account of failure of provisions.)

.   .   .   Thus the prince rode that Saturday from
the morning till it was against night, so that he came
within two little leagues of Poitiers; then the Captal
de Buch, sir Aymenon of Pumiers, the lord Bartholo-
mew of Berghersh, and lord Eustace d' Ambreticourt,

all these the Prince sent forth, to see if they might
know what the Frenchmen did. These knights
departed with two hundred men of arms well horsed.
They rode so far that they saw the great host of the
king of France; they saw all the fields covered with
men of arms. These Englishmen could not forbear,
but set on the tail of the French host, and cut down
many to the earth, and took divers prisoners; so that
the host began to stir and tidings thereof came to
the French king as he was entering into the city of
Poitiers. Then he returned again, and made all his
host do the same, so that Saturday it was very late
ere he was lodged in the field. The English scouts
returned again to the prince and shewed him all that
they saw and knew, and said how the French host
was a great number of people. "Well," said the
prince, "in the name of God let us now study how we
shall fight with them to our advantage." That
night the Englishmen lodged in a strong place
among hedges, vines, and bushes; and their host
was well watched, and so was the French host.

1356.—Of the order of the French before the battle of Poitiers.

Froissart ch. 160 (I. § 378).

On the Sunday in the morning the French king,
who had great desire to fight with the Englishmen,
heard his mass in his pavilion, and was houseled and
his four sons with him. After mass there came to
him the duke of Orleans, the duke of Bourbon, the
count of Ponthieu . . . . and divers others;

all these with the king went to council. Then finally
it was ordained that all manner of men should draw
into the field, and every lord display his banner
and set forth in the name of God and saint Denis.
Then trumpets blew up through the host, and every
man mounted on horseback and went into the field,
where they saw the king's banner wave with the wind.
There might have been seen great nobles with fair
harness and rich array of banners and pennons, for
there was all the flower of France. There was none
durst abide at home without he would be shamed for
ever. Then it was ordained by the advice of the
constable and marshals that three lines of battle
should be made ; and in each division sixteen
thousand men of arms. . . . The first battle the
duke of Orleans was to govern with thirty-six banners
and twice as many pennons ; the second the duke of
Normandy and his two brethren the lord Louis and
the lord John ; the third the king himself. And
while these battles were setting in array, the king
called to him the lord Eustace Ribeaumont, the lord
John of Landas and the lord Guiscard of Beaujeu,
and said to them, " Sirs, ride on before to see the
dealing of the Englishmen, and mark well what
number they be, and by what means we may fight
with them, either on foot or a horseback." These
three knights rode forth. The king was on a white
charger and cried aloud to his men, " Sirs, among you
when you are at Paris, at Chartres, at Rouen, or at
Orleans, then you do threaten the Englishmen and
desire to be in arms out against them. Now you are

come thereto ; I shall now shew you them ; now shew forth your evil will that ye bear them, and make them to rue the displeasures and damages they have done you, for without doubt we shall fight with them." Such as heard him said, " Sir, in God's name so be it ; that would we see gladly." Herewith the three knights returned again to the king, who demanded of them tidings. Then sir Eustace of Ribeaumont answered for all, and said, " Sir, we have seen the Englishmen, and, by estimation, they are two thousand men at arms, and four thousand archers, and fifteen hundred others ; howbeit they are in a strong place. And, as far as we can imagine, they are arranged in one body ; howbeit they are wisely ordered, and along the way they have fortified strongly the hedges and bushes ; one part of their archers are along by the hedge, so that none can go nor ride that way but must pass by them. And that way must you go, if you purpose to fight with them. In this hedge there is but one entry and one issue, through which perchance but four horsemen may ride abreast ; at the end of this hedge, where no man can go nor ride, there be men of arms afoot and archers before them in manner of a harrow, so that they will not be lightly discomfited." " Well," said the king, "what will you then counsel us to do?" Sir Eustace said, "Sir, let us all be afoot except three hundred men of arms well horsed, of the best in your host and most hardy, to the intent they may somewhat break and open the archers ; and then your divisions to follow on quickly afoot, and so to fight with their men of arms hand to hand. This is the best advice that I can give you ; if any other think any other way better, let him speak." The king said, "Thus shall it be done."

1356.—How the cardinal of Périgord treated to make agreement between the French king and the prince before the battle of Poitiers.

Froissart, ch. 161 (I. § 380.)

When the French king's lines of battle were ordered and every lord under his banner among his own men, then it was commanded that every man should cut his spear to five feet long, and every man put off his spurs. Thus as they were ready to approach, the cardinal of Périgord came in great haste to the king ; he came the same morning from Poitiers ; he kneeled down to the king and held up his hands, and desired him for God's sake a little to abstain setting forward till he had spoken with him. Then he said, "Sir, ye have here all the flower of your realm against a handful of Englishmen in comparison to your company. And, sir, if you may have them accorded to you without battle, it shall be more profitable and honourable to have them by that manner, rather than to adventure so noble chivalry as you have here present. Sir, I beg of you in the name of God and humility that I may ride to the prince, and shew him what danger you have him in." The king said, "It pleaseth me well ; but return again shortly." The cardinal departed, and diligently he rode to the prince, who was among his men afoot. Then the cardinal alighted, and came to the prince, who received him courteously. Then the cardinal, after his salutation made, said, " Certainly, fair son, if you and your counsel consider rightly the puissance of the French king, you will suffer me to treat to make a peace between you, if I may." The prince, who was young and lusty, said, " Sir, the honour of me and of my people saved, I would gladly fall to any reasonable way."

Then the cardinal said, " Sir, you say well, and I shall accord you if I can ; for it should be great pity if so many noble men and others as be here on both parties should come together by battle." . . . . . That Sunday all the day the cardinal travailed in riding from the one host to the other gladly to agree them. . . . . . In the mean-season that the cardinal rode thus between the hosts, in trust to do some good, certain knights of France and of England both rode forth the same Sunday, because it was truce for that day, to coast the hosts and to behold the dealing of their enemies. So it fortuned that the lord John Chandos rode the same day coasting the French host ; and in like manner the lord of Clermont, one of the French marshals, had ridden forth and viewed the state of the English host ; and as these two knights returned towards their hosts they met together, and each of them bore one manner of device ; a blue lady embroidered in a sunbeam above on their apparel. Then the lord Clermont said : " Chandos,

how long have you taken on you to bear my device?"
"Nay, you bear mine," said Chandos, "for it is as
well mine as yours." "I deny that," said Clermont,
"and if it were not for the truce this day between
us, I should make it good on you forthwith that
you have no right to bear my device." "Ha! sir,"
said Chandos, "you shall find me to-morrow ready
to meet you, and to prove by feat of arms that it
is as well mine as yours." Then Clermont said,
"Chandos, these be well the words of you Englishmen, for you can devise nothing new, but all that
you see is good and fair." So they departed
without any more doing, and each of them returned
to their host.

The cardinal of Périgord could in no wise that
Sunday make any agreement between the parties;
and when it was near night he returned to Poitiers.
. . . . . . All the prince's company passed
not eight thousand men of one and other, and
the Frenchmen were sixty thousand fighting men,
whereof there were more than three thousand
knights.

1356, Sept. 19.—Of the battle of Poitiers between the prince of Wales and the French king.

Froissart, ch. 162 (I. § 384).

When the prince saw that he should have battle,
and that the cardinal was gone without any peace
or truce making, and saw that the French king
did not set but little store by him, he said then
to his men, "Now, sirs, though we are but a

how lo
" Nay,
well n
" and
us, I
you h
said (
to m
is as
" Ch
men,
you
with
to tl
T
Sun
and

. .

not
the
wh
kni

13

an
or
di
to

small company as in regard to the puissance of
our enemies, let us not be abashed therefor, for
the victory lieth not in the multitude of people,
but where as God will send it. If it fortune that
the day be ours, we shall be the most honoured
people of all the world; and if we die in our
right quarrel, I have the king my father and my
brethren, and also you have good friends and
kinsmen, these shall avenge us. Therefore, sirs,
for God's sake I require you to do your devoir
this day; for if God be pleased and Saint George,
this day shall see me a good knight." These
words and such others that the prince spake comforted all his people. The lord sir John Chandos
that day never went from the prince: nor also the
lord James Audley, for a great while; but when
he saw that they should needs fight, he said to
the prince, "Sir, I have served always truly my
lord your father and you also, and shall do as long
as I live; I say this because I made once a vow
that the first battle that either the king your father
or any of his children should be at, how that I
would be one of the first setters-on, or else to
die in the pain. Therefore, I require your grace
as in regard for any service that ever I did to the
king your father or to you, that you will give me
licence to depart from you and to set myself there
as I may accomplish my vow." The prince accorded
to his desire and said, "Sir James, God give you
this day that grace to be the best knight of all
others," and so took him by the hand. Then the

knight departed from the prince, and went to the
foremost front of all the battles, only accompanied
with four squires who promised not to fail him.
This lord James was a right sage and a valiant
knight, and by him was much of the host ordained
and governed the day before. . . . .   Then the
battle began on all parts, and the lines of the
marshals of France approached, and they set forth
that were appointed to break the ranks of the
archers. They entered a-horse-back into the way,
where the great hedges were on both sides set full
of archers. As soon as the men of arms entered,
the archers began to shoot on both sides, and did
slay and hurt horses and knights. So that the
horses, when they felt the sharp arrows, would
in no wise go forward, but drew back and flung
and took on so fiercely that many of them fell
on their masters, so that for press they could not
rise again. Insomuch that the marshal's division
could never come at the prince. Certain knights
and squires that were well mounted passed through
the archers, and thought to approach to the prince,
but they could not. The lord James Audley, with
four squires, was in the front of that battle, and
there did marvels in arms ; and by great prowess
he came and fought with sir Arnold d'Andrehen
under his own banner, and there they fought long
together, and sir Arnold was there sore handled.
The division of the marshals began to disorder
by reason of the shot of the archers with the
aid of the men of arms, who came in among

them, and slew them, and did what they list.
And there was the lord Arnold D'Andrehen taken
prisoner by other men than by sir James Audley, or
by his four squires, for that day he never took
prisoner, but always fought and went on his enemies.
Also, on the French part, the lord John Clermont
fought under his own banner as long as he could
endure ; but there he was beaten down and could
not be relieved nor ransomed, but was slain without
mercy ; some said it was because of the words that
he had the day before to sir John Chandos. So
within a short space the marshal's divisions were
discomfited, for they fell one upon another and
could not go forth ; and the Frenchmen that were
behind and could not get forward recoiled back, and
came on the battalion of the duke of Normandy,
which was great and thick and afoot ; but
anon they began to open behind. For when they
knew that the marshal's division was discomfited
they took their horses and departed, he that might
best. Also they saw a rout of Englishmen coming
down a little mountain on horseback and many
archers with them, who broke in on the side of the
duke of Orleans' division. True to say, the archers
did their company that day great advantage, for they
shot so thick that the Frenchmen wist not on what
side to take heed ; and little and little the Englishmen won ground on them. And when the men of
arms of England saw that the marshal's division
was discomfited, and that the duke's division began to
disorder and open, they leapt then on their horses

which they had ready by them. Then they assembled together, and cried "Saint George for Guienne!" And the lord Chandos said to the prince, "Sir, take your horse and ride forth; this enterprise is yours; God is this day in your hands; get us to the French king's division, for there lieth all the sore of the matter. I think verily by his valiantness he will not fly; I trust we shall have him, by the grace of God and Saint George, so he be well fought withal. And sir, I heard you say that this day I should see you a good knight." The prince said, "Let us go forth; you shall not see me this day turn back." Then he said, "Advance banner in the name of God and of Saint George!" The knight that bore it did his commandment. There was then a sore battle and a perilous, and many a man overthrown; and he that was once down could not be raised again, without great succour and aid. As the prince rode and entered in among his enemies, he saw on his right hand, in a little bush lying dead, the lord Robert of Durazzo and his banner by him, and ten or twelve of his men about him. Then the prince said to two of his squires and to three archers, "Sirs, take the body of this knight on a shield and bear him to Poitiers, and present him from me to the Cardinal of Périgord and say how I salute him by this token." And this was done. The prince was informed that the cardinal's men were on the field against him, howbeit without the knowledge or consent of their master, the which was not according to the right order of arms; for men of the Church, that come and go for treaty of peace, ought not by reason to bear arms nor to fight for either of the parties; they ought to be indifferent. And because these men had done so, the prince was displeased with the cardinal, and therefore he sent unto him his nephew, the lord Robert of Durazzo, dead. . . . . .

The lord James Audley with the aid of his four squires fought always in the chief of the battle. He was sore hurt in the body and in the visage; as long as his breath served him, he fought. At last, at the end of the battle, his four squires took and brought him out of the field, and laid him under a hedge-side for to refresh him. And they unarmed him and bound up his wounds as well as they could. On the French part, king John was that day a full right good knight; if the fourth part of his men had done their devoirs as well as he did, the day had been his by all likelihood.

1356.—How king John was taken prisoner at the battle of Poitiers.

Froissart, ch. 163 (I. § 392).

Often times the adventures of love and of war are more fortunate and marvellous than any man can think or wish. Truly this battle, the which was near to Poitiers, in the fields of Beaumont and Maupertuis, was right great and perilous, and many deeds of arms there were done, the which came not all to knowledge. The fighters on both parties endured much pain. King John with his own hands

did that day marvels in arms; he had an axe in his
hands, wherewith he defended himself and fought in
the breaking of the press. The chase endured to
the gates of Poitiers; there were many slain and
beaten down, horse and man, for they of Poitiers
closed their gates and would suffer none to enter.
Wherefore in the street before the gate was horrible
murder, men hurt and beaten down. The Frenchmen yielded themselves as far off as they might
know an Englishman; there were divers English
archers that had four, five, or six prisoners.
. . . . Then there was a great press
to take the king, and such as knew him cried
" Sir, yield you, or else you are but dead !" There
was a knight of Saint Omer retained in wages with
the king of England, called sir Denis Morbeque,·
who had served the Englishmen five years before,
because in his youth he had forfeited the realm of
France for a murder that he did at Saint Omer. It
happened so well for him that he was next to the
king when they were about to take him. He stept
forth into the press, and by strength of his body and
arms he came to the French king, and said in good
French, "Sir, yield you." The king beheld the
knight and said, "To whom shall I yield me ?
Where is my cousin the prince of Wales ? If I
might see him, I would speak with him." Denis
answered and said, " Sir, he is not here, but yield
you to me, and I shall bring you to him." " Who
are you ?" quoth the king. "Sir," quoth he, " I
am Denis of Morbeque, a knight of Artois, but I

serve the king of England because I am banished
the realm of France, and I have forfeited all that
I had there." Then the king gave him his right
gauntlet, saying " I yield me to you." There was
a great press about the king, for every man was anxious
to say " I have taken him ;" so that the king
could not go forward with his young son, the lord
Philip, with him by cause of the press. The prince
of Wales, who was courageous and cruel as a lion,
took that day great pleasure to fight and to chase his
enemies. The lord John Chandos who was with
him all that day never left him, and never took
heed of taking of any prisoner. Then, at end of the
battle, he said to the prince, " Sir, it were good that
you rested here, and set your banner ahigh in this
bush, that your people may draw hither, for they be
sore spread abroad ; I can see no more banners
nor pennons of the French party. Wherefore, sir,
rest and refresh you, for you are sore chafed." Then
the prince's banner was set up ahigh on a bush, and
trumpets and clarions began to sound. Then the
prince did take off his basenet ; and the knights for
his body and those of his chamber were ready about
him and a red pavilion pitched. And when the
two marshals were come to the prince he demanded
of them if they knew any tidings of the French king.
They answered and said, " Sir, we hear none of
certainty, but we think verily he is either dead or
taken, for he is not gone out of the battle." Then
the prince said to the earl of Warwick and to sir
Reynold Cobham, " Sirs, I require you to go forth

and see what you can know, that at your return you
may show me the truth." These two lords took
their horses and departed from the prince, and rode
up a little hill to look about them. Then they
perceived a flock of men of arms coming together
right wearily. There was the French king afoot in
great peril; for Englishmen and Gascons were his
masters. They had taken him from sir Denis
Morbeque perforce, and such as were most of force
said, " I have taken him." " Nay," quoth another,
"I have taken him;" so they strove which should have
him. Then the French king to escape that peril
said, " Sirs, strive not, lead me courteously and my
son to my cousin the prince, and strive not for my
taking. For I am a lord great enough to make you all
rich." The king's words somewhat appeased them,
howbeit ever as they went they made riot and brawled
for the taking of the king. When the two aforesaid
lords saw and heard that noise and strife among
them, they came to them and said, " Sirs, what is
the matter that you strive for ?" " Sirs," said one of
them, " it is for the French king, who is here taken
prisoner ; and there be more than ten knights and
squires that challenge the taking of him and his
son." Then the two lords entered into the press,
and caused every man to draw aback, and commanded
them in the prince's name, on pain of their heads, to
make no more noise and to approach the king no
nearer without they were commanded. Then every
man gave room to the lords, and they alighted and
did their reverence to the king, and so brought him
and his son in peace and rest to the Prince of Wales.

1356.—How the prince made a supper to the French king the same day of the battle.

Froissart, ch. 168. (I. § 397.)

The same day of the battle at night the prince made a supper in his lodging to the French king and to the most part of the great lords that were prisoners. And always the prince served before the king as humbly as he could, and would not sit at the king's board for any desire that the king could make; but he said he was not sufficient to sit at the table with so great a prince as the king was. Then he said to the king, "Sir, for God's sake make no evil nor heavy cheer, though God this day did not consent to follow your will. For, sir, surely the king my father shall bear you as much honour and good will as he may do, and shall accord with you so reasonably that you shall ever be friends together after. And, sir, I think you ought to rejoice, though the day be not as you would have had it, for this day you have now the high renown of prowess, and have passed this day in valiantness all other of your party. Sir, I say this not to mock you, for all that be on our party, that saw every man's deeds, are plainly accorded by true sentence to give you the prize and chaplet."

Therewith the Frenchmen began to murmur, and said among themselves, how the prince had spoken nobly, and that by all estimation he should prove a noble man if God sent him life and to persevere in such good fortune.

1357.—How the prince conveyed the French king from Bordeaux into England.

Froissart, ch. 173.   (I. § 403.)

Then he took the sea and certain lords of Gascony with him.   The French king was in a vessel by himself to be more at his ease.   There went with them two hundred men of arms and two thousand archers. For it was shewed the prince that the three estates, by whom the realm of France was governed, had laid in Normandy and Crotoy two great armies to the intent to meet with him, and to get the French king out of his hands if they might; but there were no such that appeared.   And yet they were on the sea eleven days, and on the twelfth day they arrived at Sandwich.   Then they issued out of their ships, and lay all that night and tarried there two days to refresh them, and on the third day they rode to Canterbury. When the king of England knew of their coming he commanded them of London to prepare themselves and their city to receive such a man as the French king was.   Then they of London arrayed themselves by companies, and the chief masters' clothing different from the others.   At Saint Thomas of Canterbury the French king and the prince made their offerings, and there tarried a day, and then rode to Rochester. And they tarried there that day, and the next day to Dartford, and the fourth day to London, where they were honourably received, and so they were in every good town as they passed.   The French king rode through London on a white charger well-apparelled, and the prince on a little black hobby by him.   Thus he was conveyed along the city till he came to the Savoy, the which house pertained to the heritage of the Duke of Lancaster. There the French king kept his house a long season, and thither came to see him the king and the queen of England oftentimes, and made him great feast and cheer. Anon after, by the commandment of pope Innocent the Sixth, there came into England the lord cardinal of Périgord and the lord Nicholas, cardinal of Urgel. They treated for a peace between the two kings, but they could bring nothing to effect. But at last by good means they procured a truce between the two kings and all their allies, to endure till the feast of Saint John the Baptist, in the year of our Lord God 1359. And out of this truce was excepted the lord Philip of Navarre and his allies, the countess of Montfort and the duchy of Bretagny. Anon after the French king was moved from the Savoy to the castle of Windsor, and all his household. And went a-hunting and a-hawking there about at his pleasure, and the lord Philip, his son, with him. And all the other prisoners abode still at London, and went to see the king at their pleasure.

1360.—The treaty of Brétigny.

(The truce came to an end at the beginning of 1359, but the Dauphin and the French estates would not accept the English terms, and war was renewed. Edward gathered a larger army than ever before, marched in November from Calais to Rheims, which he failed to reduce, and then on towards Burgundy, forcing its duke to purchase neutrality. Returning, he encamped outside Paris, not venturing upon an assault; and at last, in May, terms of peace were agreed upon.

Froissart, ch. 212 (1. § 474).

   . . . "Our brother of France and his said son are bound and promise to deliver and to leave to us, our heirs and successors for ever, the counties, cities, towns, castles, fortresses, lands, isles, rents, revenues and other things as followeth, beside that we have and hold already in Guienne and Gascony, to possess perpetually by us and by our heirs and successors, all that is in demesne and all that is in fee, by the time and manner hereafter declared: that is to say, the castle and county of Poitiers, and all the lands and country of Poitou, with the fee of Thouars and the lands of Belleville; the city and castle of Saintes, and all the lands and county of Saintonge, on both sides the river of Charente, with the town and fortress of Rochelle and their appurtenances; and the city and castle of Agen and the country of Agenois; the city, town, and castle of Perigord, and all the country thereto belonging; the city and castle of Limoges and the land and country of Limousin; the city and castle of Cahors; the castle and country of Tarbes; the lands, country, and county of Bigorre; the county, country, and land of Gaure; the city and castle of Angoulême and all the country thereto pertaining; the city, town, and castle of Rodez, and the county and country of Rouergne. And if there be in the duchy of Guienne any lords, as the earl of Foix, the earl of Armagnac, the earl of Lisle, the viscount of Carmaine, the earl of Perigord, the

viscount of Limoges, or other, holding any lands within the foresaid bounds, they shall do homage to us and all other services due and accustomed. . . Also the castle and town of Calais; the castle, town, and seignory of Merle; the towns, castles, and seignories of Sangates, Coulougne, Ham, Walles, and Oye; with the lands, woods, marshes, rivers, rents, revenues, seignories, advowsons of churches, and all other appurtenances and places. . . . .
. . . . And it hath been agreed that our said brother and his eldest son should renounce all manner of sovereignty, resort, and rights, that he should have of any of them or for them; and that we should hold them as his neighbour, without any resort or sovereignty to our said brother or to the realm of France; and all the right that our said brother hath in the aforesaid things, he yieldeth and transferreth them to us perpetually. And also it is agreed that likewise we and our said son expressly renounce all things that ought not to be delivered to us by the said treaty, and specially of the name and right to the crown of France and to the realm and homage and sovereignty and domain of the duchy of Normandy, of the county of Touraine, and of the counties of Anjou and Maine, and the sovereignty and homage of the duchy of Brittany; except the right of the earl of Montfort, that he ought or might have in the duchy and county of Brittany, the which we reserve, and by express words put clean out of this our treaty, saving that we and our said brother when we come to Calais shall order that matter and settle a peace and concord between the earl Montfort and

APPENDIX.

I. THE AUTHORITIES.

1. The greater number of the extracts in this book are taken from *Lord Berners' Translation of the Chronicle of Froissart*. Jehan Froissart was born at Valenciennes about 1337, and entered very early the service of his countrywoman Philippa of Hainault, the queen of Edward III. Upon her death in 1369 he returned to his native land, and it was then that, at the request of Philippa's brother-in-law, Robert of Namur, Froissart wrote the first version of his chronicle. The narrative of events before 1356 is based upon and, in the earlier part, verbally identical with the chronicle of Jehan le Bel, whose work is mentioned below; it is to this writer, and not to Froissart, that we are really indebted for some of the finest and best known passages, such as those describing the death-bed of Robert Bruce, and the siege of Calais. Froissart is never more than a chronicler; he is never a critical historian; and therefore, as was natural with his surroundings, this first version, which has alone become generally known, gives only the English version of the disputes between England and France and of the military operations. In reading his stirring narrative, this partiality for the English must never be forgotten.

Two manuscripts, those of Amiens and Valenciennes, give a later version of Book I. It seems to have been written about

1376, when Froissart was under the patronage of two firm adherents of France, Wenceslas of Brabant and Guy of Blois, and the ties binding him to England were all broken. This second narrative, in consequence, presents the French version of the events, differing frequently from the earlier account. And a still later version is preserved in one manuscript in Rome. Froissart had become a canon of Chimay, and is said to have died in 1410.

Froissart never attempts to examine evidence; his later versions are not improved and corrected editions of the earlier, but simply "other accounts." Each is but a well-written reproduction of the story told by the men around him; and, therefore, the editor has not scrupled to give the narrative as it is presented in the better known version, although it is somewhat partisan in character.

An additional reason for so doing is that he is thus enabled to make use of the vigorous sixteenth-century translation by *Lord Berners*, which reproduces the naive simplicity of the original far more than any modern translator could hope to do. John Bourchier, Lord Berners, who was born some sixty years after Froissart's death, it is said in 1467, served Henry VII. and Henry VIII. in war and diplomacy; and, after being for many years governor of Calais, died in that town in 1532. His translation of Froissart, undertaken at the command of Henry VIII., was printed by Pynson in black letter in 1523, and reprinted in 1812. The only changes that have been made are such verbal alterations as are necessary to make the sense clear. The references at the head of each extract are to the chapter in which it will be found in Berners, and, in brackets, to book and section in the only critical edition of Froissart that has appeared, that of M. Luce, for the Société de l'histoire de France.

2. Where the account is verbally or in the main derived from

Jehan le Bel, a reference is also given to the edition of that
writer by M. Polain (1863).   Of Jehan le Bel's personal history
very little is known, save that he was of a patrician family of
Liège, and was born about the end of the thirteenth century;
that with his brother he accompanied John of Hainault to
England, and took part in the expeditions against the Scots
in the early years of Edward, so that the narrative is here that
of an eyewitness; and that he became a canon of Liège, and
died in 1370.

3. A great contrast to the detailed and picturesque narrative
of Froissart is presented by *Adam of Murimuth*, who wrote
short and simple annals of his own time from 1303 to 1346.   He
had unusual facilities for obtaining information, since he was
employed in important diplomatic missions by Edward II. and
Edward III., gaining as reward canonries at Hereford and
London.   His information, though very concise, is extremely
valuable; an anonymous *Continuatio*, which is equally useful,
carries on the narrative to 1380.   His chronicle was edited by
Mr. Hog for the English Historical Society in 1846.

4. Similar in character is the work of *Robert of Avesbury*,
whose "History of the wonderful deeds of Edward III." has
been only once printed, by Thomas Hearne in 1720.   The
writer describes himself as registrar of the archbishop's court at
Canterbury.   His work is more detailed than that of Murimuth
or his continuator, and is equally trustworthy.   Unfortunately it
breaks off before the battle of Poitiers.

5. *Henry of Knighton*, a canon at Leicester, in the second
half of the 15th century, had access to the papers of the earls of
Leicester of the house of Lancaster, and follows with special
interest and pride the actions of Henry of Derby, afterwards
duke of Lancaster,   He becomes independent in his narrative
about the middle of the century; there is a break between 1367

and 1377; and then he continues his work to 1395. We owe to him many interesting notices of the social life of the time.

6. *The Chronicle of Lanercost*, the best authority for Border history and for the Scotch wars of the period, seems to have been given this name by mistake; it was more probably written by a Franciscan of the convent of Carlisle. The author gives full accounts of the campaigns and important battles, written with considerable vigour and rough humour; his sympathies are, of course, entirely English. The chronicle was edited by Mr. Stevenson for the Maitland and Bannatyne clubs in 1839.

7. Two interesting extracts have been made from a popular manual for confessors and the devout, called the *Ayenbite of Inwyt*, which has been edited by Mr. Morris. This is a translation made by Dan Michel, a Kentish monk, about 1340, of an earlier French treatise, and illustrates excellently the economic ideas of the time.

Besides these sources of information, use has been made of *Political Poems*, ed. Wright, the *Munimenta Gildhallae*, ed. Riley, the *Gesta Abbatum Monasterii S. Albani*, ed. Riley, all in the Rolls' Series; and of the two great collections, the *Statutes of the Realm*, and *Rymer's Fœdera* (ed. Record Commission). The illustrations of the *Skirmishing on the Tyne*, and of the battles of *Crecy* and *Poitiers* are from a 15th Century MS. of Froissart, preserved in the Paris *Bibliothèque Nationale* (MS. n. 2643).

2. THE ROYAL FAMILY.

Henry III.

Edward I.

Edward II. = Isabella of France, who died 1357.
Thomas earl of Norfolk, d. 1338.
Edmund earl of Kent, executed 1330.
Edmund.

Joan = Edward of Woodstock
Thomas earl of Lancaster.
Henry earl of Lancaster, Leicester, Derby, etc., d. 1345.

Edward III.
John of Eltham earl of Cornwall, d. 1336.
Eleanore = Reinald of Guelders.
Joan = David Bruce, d. 1362.
Henry earl of Derby, 1345 earl of Lancaster, d. 1360.

Blanche = John of Gaunt.

Edward of Woodstock the Black Prince, Joan of Kent 1361, d. 1376.
Lionel of Antwerp, duke of Clarence, d. 1368.
John of Gaunt, duke of Lancaster, d. 1399.
Edmund of Langley, duke of York, d. 1402.
Thomas of Woodstock, duke of Gloucester, d. 1397.

3. THE FRENCH SUCCESSION.

Philip III.
1270-1285.

Philip IV. the Fair, 1285-1314.　　　　Charles of Valois.

Louis X. 1314-1316.　　Philip V. 1316-1322.　　Charles IV. 1322-1328.　　Isabella=Edward II.　　Philip VI. of Valois. 1328-1350.

Joan=King of Navarre.　　　　　　　　　　Edward III.　　　　John. 1350-1364.

Charles the Bad, King of Navarre.　　　　　　　　　　　　Charles V. 1364-1380.

The three sons of Philip IV. having died without male heirs, Edward claimed the throne as the son of a daughter of Philip IV., against Philip of Valois, the son of a brother of Philip IV. But it had been long held that the succession to the French throne was regulated by what was called "the Salic law," which excluded females or their descendants. Edward declared that this only excluded females themselves (Joan of Navarre and the daughters of Philip IV.'s, sons), and that he had a better claim than their male children because he was born during the lifetime of the grandfather.

4. THE SUCCESSION TO BRITTANY.

Mary=(1) Duke ARTHUR=(2) Yoland of Montfort.

John III.   Guy.   *John* IV.=*Joan* of Flanders.
d. 1341.   Earl *of Montfort*,
                    d. 1345.
    Joan=*Charles of Blois*,
     son of a sister of
   Philip VI. of France,
       d. 1364.

5. THE EMPEROR LEWIS IV. OF BAVARIA.

Lewis of Bavaria, who had been elected emperor in 1314, was engaged during the greater part of his life in a struggle with the popes, who were supported and prompted by the French kings. In 1324 pope John XXII. had put him under the ban and declared him deposed ; in 1328 Lewis marched to Rome where he was crowned emperor, and set up an anti-pope. Edward seems to have thought it possible to make use of the imperial authority to obtain the support of all the princes of the Netherlands and of north-western Germany ; but the campaign of 1340 proved that he could only expect assistance from them in proportion to the payments he could make them, and he soon dropped the title of vicar which had proved useless.

6. TAXATION UNDER EDWARD III.

By the *Confirmation of the Charters* in 1297 Edward 1. had promised for himself and his heirs that henceforth they would not take " such manner of aids, tasks, or prises " as had been complained of, but " by the common assent of the realm," and that they would not take any tax on wool "without their common assent." But this left open to the king two ways of obtaining money without parliamentary sanction. There was first his right to *tallage* his demesne, (including most of the towns in the kingdom,) which belonged to him as landlord. Three instances of the exercise of this right are found after 1297, one in each of the reigns of Edward I., Edward II., and Edward III.; but by the statute of 1340 Edward III. was understood to give up the claim, and it was never afterwards put forward. The same statute was also explicit enough to deprive the king of another means of raising money which it had been urged did not violate the spirit of the Confirmation, namely by *voluntary grant of customs on the part of the merchants ;* but it was necessary to expressly prohibit this practice in 1362, and again in 1371.

7. CHARLES OF NAVARRE.

Charles *the Bad* (a title which his cruelty early won for him) was the son of Joan the daughter of Louis X. of France. He succeeded in 1349 to the kingdom of Navarre and to the county of Evreux in Normandy ; and in 1352 king John gave him his daughter in marriage. His power in Normandy, his great ability, and his claim to the French throne through his mother, made him so dangerous that John would have done well to make a close alliance with him ; but instead of doing this, he refused to carry out certain promises which had been made to Joan of Navarre, and treated the young Charles with scant consideration. In revenge Charles caused the king's favourite, the constable,

Charles de la Cerda, to whom he attributed this illtreatment, to be assassinated in January 1354. Civil war was imminent; but, next month, John was induced to make terms with Charles and go through the ceremony of reconciliation. John wished only to gain time and began to gather troops. Charles, thereupon, made overtures to Edward and arranged to receive an English force at Cherbourg. Under the pressure of necessity John again in September accepted his conditions; and the English landing in Normandy was prevented at the last moment.

CONTENTS.

PAGE

APPENDIX.

CPSIA information can be obtained
at www.ICGtesting.com
Printed in the USA
BVOW06*1634041017

496748BV00008B/39/P